*Just a Note to Say...*

# Just a Note to Say...

the perfect
words for every
occasion

## FLORENCE ISAACS

Clarkson Potter/Publishers
New York

Published in the United States by Clarkson
Potter/Publishers, an imprint of the Crown
Publishing Group, a division of Random House, Inc.,
New York.
www.crownpublishing.com
www.clarksonpotter.com
Clarkson N. Potter is a trademark and Potter
and colophon are registered trademarks
of Random House, Inc.
Originally published in different form by
Clarkson Potter/Publishers, an imprint
of the Crown Publishing Group, a division
of Random House, Inc., New York, in 1995.
Library of Congress Cataloging-in-Publication Data
Isaacs, Florence.
Just a note to say: the perfect words for every
occasion/Florence Isaacs.—1st rev. ed.
1. Letter writing. 2. English language—Rhetoric.
3. Interpersonal communication. I. Title.
PE1483.I83 2005
808.6—dc22                    2005010611
ISBN-13: 978-0-307-23665-4
ISBN-10: 0-307-23665-X
Printed in the United States of America
Design by Jennifer K. Beal
10 9 8 7 6 5 4 3 2 1
First Revised Edition

# Contents

## PART 3

## Writing Notes for Difficult Moments 101

## PART 4

## Writing Notes for Other Occasions 137

# ❄ *Preface* ❄

I had no idea when *Just a Note to Say . . .* was first published that it would strike such a responsive chord in readers. In this updated and expanded edition, I've kept the special bond clearly in mind. Much has changed in our lives and in the world since I initially completed the book. The shifts are reflected in the attention I've devoted to electronic communication and in the new ideas and sample notes added throughout this edition. The insights and tips that make note writing easy, yet meaningful, remain—but there are more of them.

When I first started to explore in depth the subject of notes for this book, I did not know that the project would become a process of discovery. Yet each chapter held surprises.

As I talked to people about various occasions, inquiring about their feelings and attitudes, I often found their responses a revelation. Many would say, "I've never thought much about birthdays (or graduations or anniversaries) before"—then proceed to share poignant insights. They spoke of deeply felt emotions and their voices became some of the highlights of this book.

Men could be just as thoughtful and expressive as women—and often more so. Some of the sweetest, most touching words came from husbands, sons, brothers, or friends who felt genuinely moved by the occasions that inspired their notes.

Some of my preconceived notions about what constitutes a good note changed, as well. As I examined the underlying meaning of (and issues involved in) each occasion, I discovered that notes that had seemed ideal to me at the start of this project looked different later on. Words that meant well and sounded right on target could sometimes have unintended implications and actually be inappropriate.

Psychologists, social workers, and other professionals helped me to explore complex issues in the first edition and write an infinitely richer book. I thank them all, especially Renee Warshofsky-Altholz, CSW, ACSW; Rabbi Shelley Kovar Becker; Bernice R. Berk, PhD; Linda Carter, PhD; Ricki Fier, RN, MS, CS; Reverend Elizabeth G. Maxwell; Diane Rosenstein, ACSW; Michael Shernoff, ACSW; Mary-Ellen Siegel, MSW; and W. Daniel Smith.

I also thank many of my colleagues, members of The American Society of Journalists and Authors, for their exceptional support.

P.S. If you'd like to share your own experiences with finding the right words—or meaningful notes you've received—I'd love to hear from you. Please contact me through my Web site at www.florenceisaacs.com or e-mail fisaacs@florenceisaacs.com. You can also write to me: Florence Isaacs, c/o Clarkson Potter/Publishers, 1745 Broadway, New York, NY 10019.

# Part 1

## The Power of Notes

# One

## Making Connections in Changing Times

When I had my first baby, I received a gift at the hospital with a note that read, "To Jonathan: We're so glad you're here." I'll always remember that note—and the person who sent it. This baby was one I feared I'd never have. I had tried to become pregnant, unsuccessfully, for three years and had watched other women wheeling baby carriages, feeling waves of despair that I would never have the chance.

Then, magically, a few days before I was due for an appointment with yet another infertility specialist, I received the good news—I was pregnant. Though my doctor warned me that things could yet go wrong—I could miscarry—I *willed* it to be all right, and it was. When I saw my beautiful, perfect son for the first time, all the heartache and doubt and fear that I'd never have a child was swept away and I felt an exquisite joy. This was not just a baby, this was the most wanted baby in the world.

That brief but meaningful note let me know that someone else understood my happiness. Oddly enough, the writer of the note was not a close friend, but at the moment I read her words, we shared a special bond. She had acknowledged how much this child meant to me.

If she had simply called or signed her name to a printed card, I'd have appreciated it. But, as I learned that day, there's nothing like a personal note to make you feel touched and remembered. That fact remains truer than ever today. In this age of impersonal technology, a handwritten note makes a human connection that is as valuable as the sentiments expressed.

## CHANGING TIMES

In other centuries, people *had* to write notes and letters to stay in touch with friends, family, and others important to them. On a trip to Mount Vernon, I learned that George Washington wrote almost forty thousand letters during his lifetime.

Of course, technology provides many other ways of communicating today. You turn on your speedy computer and push a button to e-mail your friends, family members, and others at work or in the community. You can contact anyone on the phone from a train, in your car, or virtually anywhere—even walking down the street. You also can send an instant text message. Yet there is a difference between talking and connecting—and that's what this book is all about.

The reality is, you just don't express yourself on the telephone in the same way as you do on paper. The give-and-take of conversation interrupts the flow of thought; the immediate feedback from the other person seems to stifle free expression rather than facilitate it. That's why a phone conversation with someone you love

can sometimes feel so unsatisfying—the human connec/
incomplete.

When you speak on a cell phone, noisy distractions in public places or service interruptions add extra jarring notes. E-mail and text messages discourage you from slowing down and giving thought to what you write. The whole point is quick communication, not pensiveness and deliberation.

In these uncertain times, the need to connect seems more urgent than ever. Special occasions offer the opportunity to do that, whether you're adding a few lines to a store-bought birthday greeting or writing your own stand-alone note to say, "Hello, I miss you," to a loved one in another state or on another coast or thousands of miles away in another country.

When you write, there is no response to distract you from reaching within and exploring exactly what you feel and want to say. There is no gadget or other equipment to act as a barrier. What there *is* is an enormous sense of satisfaction. One woman told me, "When I write, I speak a whole different language. I become more open. It's as if a poetic part of me seems to spill out."

At the very same time technology has provided new modes of communication, you may be confronted with new reasons to write. Not so long ago, congratulations on a ninetieth birthday or a sixtieth wedding anniversary or becoming *great*-grandparents was rare. "Singles" didn't adopt babies. People didn't launch new careers in their fifties or sixties, or retire and later return to the workforce. Other complex scenarios, unknown two or three decades ago, may demand a personal response from you, as well. You may wish to express support to someone who has been laid off after thirty-two years with a blue-chip corporation, or who struggles with the stress of moving an elderly parent into assisted living. Or perhaps you want to send good wishes to multicultural coworkers at an important celebration or holiday.

Even for the simplest and happiest occasions, it's human to start out feeling, "I can't think of a thing to write." Awkward, uncomfortable situations present an even greater challenge. But regardless of the circumstances, words from the heart make a difference. There's no mystery to finding them, and you can master the art of writing meaningful notes even if you weren't at the top of your English class. What you write doesn't have to be poetry or run to pages; often just a personal line or two added to a greeting card speaks eloquently. Meaningful notes are not about good form, either, though sincere wishes can never be anything but good form.

Handwritten sentiments remain the gold standard and cannot be replaced by a card and just your signature. When the recipient is important to you—when you care about the impression you make—you can always relax and feel confident that you are doing the right thing by expressing warm words and personal reflections. You also know you are making an impact.

In these hurried, busy times, receiving a note or personalized card in the mail is a total experience. The person discovers among the magazines, catalogs, and bills an envelope that looks different, that feels different, that is addressed by hand. Knowing that you have taken the time and trouble to write brightens the day. Opening the envelope and reading the words bring a smile. And that note in the mail continues to make an impact. The recipient often reads it again later and perhaps even shows it to others. How often do you have the power to grab someone's complete attention during the course of the day?

A note is powerful, too, because we are assaulted by a barrage of information—much of it having little or no importance. Yet personal words on paper often are saved in a shoe box, becoming a memory to be revisited through the years—a part of a life record that may even be shown to children or grandchildren.

We're all touched by life's milestones, trials, and triumphs. The guidelines that follow will help you find words that matter for any social occasion and also clarify when e-mail is and isn't appropriate. The goal is to help you recapture the spontaneity that came naturally during childhood and get in touch with feelings that may ordinarily be brushed aside. As you become comfortable with them and put them into practice, you're likely to discover a part of yourself that has been there all the time.

# Two

## How to Express Yourself

What do you say when your mother celebrates a seventy-fifth birthday, or your spouse hits forty? What do you say to a friend who's been promoted? How do you acknowledge a new baby—when it's born three months premature and the outcome is unclear?

Situations like these arise all the time and it's easy to feel at a loss for words that are real, yet appropriate. I often felt tongue-tied myself until I started noticing notes sent to me that I especially appreciated. I began to realize how much they meant to me and what it was about them that touched me so. As I made the effort to write more effective notes to others, I discovered that the right words are surprisingly accessible when you know how to find them. There are certain general guidelines that apply to every occasion.

Good notes are gestures that celebrate, commemorate, and nurture relationships between people. They're about connecting and communicating and saying "I care." They are *not* about writing something clever, although a meaningful message may sometimes be clever as well. How can you find meaningful words? Where do you start? By tapping into the underlying significance of the occasion, the issues surrounding it, and your own authentic feelings about it and about the person you're addressing. When you do, insights emerge that help uncork the flow of genuine expression. These techniques will help inspire you.

## TARGET THE RECIPIENT

A meaningful note reflects the individual you're writing to. That's why it's important to ask, "Who is this person and what is the nature of our relationship?" Are you addressing your best friend or an acquaintance, your spouse or significant other, a parent or stepparent, a sibling, a colleague?

A good note says, "I know who you are." There are many different levels of familiarity. If you're going to write something significant, the message to a beloved uncle will sound very different from an obligatory note to someone you barely know. How you express the message can also be as important as the substance of what you say. The tone you set—how warm, friendly, affectionate, or loving you sound, the degree of distance or intimacy—depends on the relationship.

## IDENTIFY YOUR FEELINGS ABOUT THE PERSON

Because good notes reflect you as well as the recipient, the next question is, "How do I feel about this person? What are the qualities that make this person important to me?" The answers will affect what you decide to say and how you say it. Some notes involve simple politeness or courtesy, and they may occasionally be addressed to people you don't especially like or care about.

In the best of all possible worlds, we'd love all our relatives, but that isn't always the case. The truth is, you may really like a casual acquaintance and intensely dislike your brother or sister. You can't fake sentiment and you shouldn't try.

How honest can you get? It depends on the person you're addressing and the situation that inspired you to write. An anniversary note is not the place to convey negative feelings. But if you're aware of them, you can avoid sounding—and feeling—insincere, while still taking a positive approach. Be true to yourself, but be kind. Do you have a stormy relationship with your mother-in-law? When acknowledging her birthday, don't mention your anger at her comments last week, but you don't have to gush either. Just wish her a happy day.

## FOCUS ON THE OCCASION

What does this event really mean to the person—and to you? The underlying significance of the occasion plays a role in what you decide to write. For example, a twenty-fifth wedding anniversary is an achievement in these days of 50 percent divorce rates. The birth of an in vitro baby is cause for more than ordinary rejoicing for a couple who had all but given up hope of parenthood. Most moms I know consider Mother's Day a *very* important holiday and would feel crushed if they were forgotten. Realizations like these can help trigger ideas for what you want to write.

# Decide on the Message

A personal note is an opportunity to communicate wishes and sentiments. The most critical—and daunting—question is, "What do you want to say?" Many people respond with blank stares. The answer is often, "I don't know." Fortunately, there are ways to find out.

Slow down and think about the issues raised previously: the person you're writing to, the significance of the occasion, and the emotions that are stirred in you. Let your thoughts meander "as is," in a stream of consciousness—and resist the temptation to censor yourself. As adults, we tend to experience writing as "exposure" and feel that what we have to say isn't original enough, creative enough, "good enough." Afraid of criticism, we edit our thoughts. Yet there are no grades here. And don't forget, you can polish, if necessary, afterward.

As you relax, very important feelings are likely to emerge, feelings that you might ordinarily keep to yourself. This is especially true with sentiments like "I care about you" or "You're important to me" or "I love you" that might seem embarrassing to speak aloud.

Children write some of the best notes precisely because they're so open and honest and able to express sentiments in simple ways. That's why I've always saved the notes my children have written to me, such as the one my young son gave me one Valentine's Day. "This comes from the heart, not from the store," he wrote on the card he'd carefully made for me. Adults often pale at the thought of writing such words and allow commercial cards to do it for us. We have much to learn from children.

When you've found words that seem right, take a chance and pick up your pen. If it feels more comfortable, try writing on scrap paper first. Remember, you don't have to compose something lengthy and elaborate. Length does not equal impact; the simplest notes can be the most powerful.

## Devices You Can Use

Everyone needs extra help at times—even professional writers. It's also important to respect your own individual rhythms and moods. Sometimes you may not *want* to make an intimate connection— or you may feel too pressed for time to think it out. Some people or occasions don't require notes with deep meaning and you may be writing out of obligation, when your heart has nothing to do with it. Still, you can say something personal, letting people know you're thinking of them—and them alone. For all these situations, here are some tips worth trying:

### 1. Angle the message to the person.

"To someone special. Happy birthday. Love, ———," even when written by hand, is a generic message that could apply to anyone. "Why bother? It sounds as if you couldn't care less," says the man who received it. "If you're going to write, show you have *me* in mind."

This is one of the secrets of note writing. A meaningful note keys in to who the person is and reflects a special connection. At the most basic level, you personalize by using the individual's name to open the note ("Dear ———" or "To ———") or some identifying information (as in "To the sharpest lawyer I know"). Salutations such as "My dearest ———" or "Dear, sweet ———" are wonderful ways to express deep affection or admiration where appropriate. Adding greater detail, you can mention a memory of the person or of an experience you shared. This works well for everything from an anniversary to a bar mitzvah. "I remember ———" or "I'll never forget the time ———" can form the nucleus of a condolence note as well.

When you have an intimate relationship with someone, you can refer to what's going on in that person's life. A thirty-year-old fashion executive told me about the birthday note she received as she struggled with a difficult decision about a career change. A friend of hers wrote, "It's the beginning of a new decade, Jane. Do what matters to you. Happy birthday."

## 2. CONSIDER THE PERSON'S HOBBIES OR INTERESTS.

Is he or she interested in sports, books, carpentry, real estate, food, wine, travel, music? Does the person have special characteristics or "demons" (such as an addiction to shopping)? Use the subject or quality as a device for a message.

For no particular occasion, I sent a book on Matisse to an elderly artist who had become a great friend of mine. In the accompanying note I wrote, "I know how much you admire his work and immediately thought of you when I saw this at the museum. Enjoy."

When an avid doubles player was hospitalized, I wrote to her, "Are you in the wing with the tennis court? Hurry home. Our game isn't the same without you."

### 3. Key in to the gift, if there is one.

For a sixtieth birthday, someone gave a businessman a videotape of *Gone With the Wind* with a note reading, "This movie is almost as old as you are. Happy birthday with love and admiration."

Tying in with a gift is useful anytime but especially when you're writing an obligatory note and when you don't know the person. Take the second-time bride who tackled the task of writing thank-yous for scores of wedding presents. In the process, she developed a talent for communicating with obscure relatives who sent quirky gifts. To someone who sent a painted wooden duck, she wrote: "Marriage is ducky—just like your gift. We've found the perfect place for it on the shelf in the den."

### 4. Enclose clippings or photos.

Clip and send appropriate articles (on hometown news, for example) to a child away at college or in the armed forces or to a friend who has moved away. Add something handwritten, such as, "Just thought you'd be interested in this. Love, ——" with or without a comment of your own. It's a quick, easy, yet personal way to keep in touch.

Send a picture of the kids, the whole family, your home, the dog, for almost any occasion—adding a suitable personal message, of course.

### 5. Make lists.

When a coworker was ill with the flu, one woman wrote, "I wish you chicken soup, matzo balls, hot tea with honey"—all the symbols of nurturing comfort she could think of. She signed off with,

"We need you back at the office to get us organized again. Get well fast."

You can also adapt a list in a note congratulating a bridal couple (enumerating reasons why they're meant for each other) or a youngster graduating from high school or college (mentioning accomplishments), as long as you make it specific to the person and occasion. You want to sound as if you're writing to *this* particular graduate, not just anyone in the class.

6. SAY IT WITH A QUOTE.

Quotations can make a significant statement *for* you, but it's important to choose one that suits the occasion and the person and reflects you as well. For a man I know about to reach fifty, I might use:

> *No wise man ever wished to be younger.*
> *—Jonathan Swift*

Then I'd add a few personalized lines.

Get into the habit of clipping and saving anecdotes and quotes in a handy file folder so you can pull them out and use them as needed. Books of quotations, on your bookshelf at home or available at the library, can be helpful, too.

7. KEEP AN INVENTORY OF LINES THAT SAY A LOT.

Just four words—"I'm thinking of you"—speak volumes and can be used over and over again for everything from expressions of sympathy and notes to people who are very ill to birthday messages. "Be happy" or "We miss you" can be multipurpose, yet heartfelt too.

Try the words "What a" to precede a whole range of items or activities, as in "What a delicious dinner at your home last night" or "What a thoughtful gift. You remembered how I love candlesticks."

## WRITE CONVERSATIONALLY

You don't have to be someone who writes easily and regularly to touch and remember someone. You don't have to be anyone other than yourself. Just speak sincerely and in your own authentic voice. That's what will make your personal notes special.

A meaningful note sounds like the person who wrote it—real and natural. That's true even if you're writing to a stranger. Courtesy and politeness do not have to sound stiff and dull. Ask yourself, If I were talking to this person face-to-face, would I really say, "I'm heartened to hear about the birth of your child"?

Compare that to "I'm so happy to hear about your new daughter." The words become instantly more real through a conversational vocabulary and the use of specific details. If you need help, try talking out loud first and picture the person in front of you. What would you say if you met your favorite aunt on the street today and wished her a very happy birthday?

## CLOSINGS

The way you close contributes to the tone of a note, but choosing just the right sign-off can be as difficult as composing the note itself. When you're writing to someone you really care about, I think "Love" says it all. My mother often closed notes to me with a casual "Love ya," which conveys a warmth I like. "With love" and "Much love" seem a degree less intense and are useful when that's the way you feel.

What do you write, however, when your feelings don't quite reach the proportions of "love"? Let's say your father's new wife is becoming a friend. You like her, but "Love" doesn't really fit. Some people might sign off "Warmly," or "Affectionately," or "Fondly." One woman is partial to "Consider yourself hugged." If those words don't feel natural to you, try "Regards," or "Looking forward," or simply sign your name.

Whatever solution you choose, make it something that feels congenial to the person you are, the someone you're addressing, and the nature of the relationship.

When you apply these guidelines, you can begin to write notes that are truly your own for all those special times in life to be marked or celebrated. What you write will be different from what I write because we are different people, with different personalities, feelings, and relationships—and different things to say.

Whatever you write, be prepared to reap some unexpected benefits. Notes bind us together when written sincerely. It *feels good* to express your thoughts, and hearing someone say, "That was a wonderful note you sent. It meant a lot to me," gives a very special boost. Isn't there someone who would like to hear from you today?

# Three

## Etiquette for E-mail Notes and Other Electronic Communication

*I'm so happy you got the job.* Click
*How was your day at the dentist?* Click
*We'd love to come to your backyard barbecue.* Click

Technology has revolutionized the way we communicate socially, as well as on the job. And there are times when an e-mail note is an ideal choice, as in the illustrations above. At the same time, no clear rules have evolved yet for when it is (and is not) appropriate to acknowledge events or respond to special occasions via e-mail and other electronic communications. We have options available to us that never existed in the past, and it's easy to feel confused not only about what to say, but about the correct medium of communication. The wrong choice can devalue the occasion and recipient and reflect a lack of good taste, as well.

Intimacy gets lost when a computer or gadget comes between you and the person to whom you're writing. The technology supercedes the message; thoughtfulness and sincerity seem to suffer. A handwritten note says, "I've thought about you. You are important to me." It is always right, which is not true of electronic communications.

The following commonsense guidelines will help you bridge the gap between tacky and tasteful and help avoid errors of judgment. Keep them in mind to feel confident and respond appropriately every time.

## APPROPRIATE USE OF E-MAIL NOTES

E-mail and other electronic communications lack the personal touch, impact, and "class" of a handwritten note. Although an e-mail message can be printed out, there is nothing special about it. It looks like everything else on the desk, becoming anonymous. As a result, the recipient responds to it differently. I don't know anyone who treasures e-mails or saves them as keepsakes, do you?

Nevertheless, there are times when an e-mail response to an occasion or situation makes sense—and there are ways to make your electronic message as gracious and meaningful as possible. Consider e-mail:

1. WHEN YOU MIGHT NOT OTHERWISE ACKNOWLEDGE
   THE OCCASION.

It's thoughtful to say, "I'm glad for you," when something wonderful has happened to the spouse or child of someone you care about, such as acceptance at a college or a great new job. What parent wouldn't appreciate hearing from you at such times? You might not take the time to sit down to write a personal note in these instances, but it's so easy to tap out a few words—and click.

E-mail is also a way to acknowledge a small favor, such as a recommendation for a good mechanic or tailor, or to call attention to an exciting movie you've seen or a touching book you've read.

## 2. TO SUPPLEMENT A PHONE CALL OR NOTE IN THE MAIL.

I often send e-mails to a friend or relative the day before the person has important medical tests or goes in for surgery. Then I mail a handwritten get-well note or personalized card later. E-mail is also a good way to follow up cards you've sent earlier for occasions like birthdays, graduations, or holidays to people important to you—and ask for details about the special day.

## 3. TO OFFER LONG-TERM ENCOURAGEMENT.

Frequent caring words are a wonderful way to support someone engaged in an extensive project or effort, or a long recuperation, or suffering from chronic illness where there are good and bad days. Regular e-mails can also support someone grieving the loss of a loved one.

## 4. TO REACH OUT TO AN ACQUAINTANCE.

You probably wouldn't send a card to someone you've never met face-to-face or have seen in person once or twice. But you might dash off good wishes for a special occasion or express concern about illness via e-mail. Why not build goodwill at the same time you're being nice, when it's so easy and quick to do?

5. WHEN YOU WANT IMMEDIACY OR FAR-REACHING
   COMMUNICATION.

E-mail is ideal to respond to news fast, as when someone who has been trying to get pregnant finally succeeds—or someone wins the lottery.

Use e-mail to invite people to an impromptu party or a casual potluck dinner. It's also handy to send a "Save the date" message. Think twice, however, about e-mail invitations to events like baby or bridal showers. E-mail makes the occasion seem less important than an invitation in the mail. Remember, too, that some people on the guest list may not use e-mail at work or home, or they may not check it very often. The party may be over by the time they see your invitation. E-mails can also be easily deleted by mistake, causing no-shows.

By all means respond to an e-mail invitation by e-mail. Online RSVPs are fine, too, for casual events.

## THE LIMITS OF E-MAIL

E-mail is fast, efficient, and convenient. Those very advantages, however, can cause you to seem insensitive or discourteous. E-mail is not a replacement for notes or cards to people who are important to you personally or professionally.

Because e-mail is a short, hurried activity, there's no time or space for depth, the heart of a relationship. The very act of e-mail makes you less pensive. Yet you can slow yourself down and make a social e-mail as personal as possible. Try visualizing a crisp correspondence card or note sheet in front of you. Take a minute to think about what to write. The examples and tips in the chapters ahead will help steer you to the right words online, as well as when you write a note by hand.

## E-CARDS

E-cards have become popular, especially among the young, to acknowledge birthdays and other occasions. Some people enjoy receiving them, feeling "Everyone is busy." Many others consider them a poor replacement for a card or note in the mail—and may even feel insulted by them. People can push the delete button on an e-card because it's clogging the system. Comments I've heard include:

"I wouldn't send an e-card to someone I'm close to. I'd kick my sister if she sent me one."

"E-cards smack of a last-minute thought. You went online, said 'This is cute,' and clicked. I feel much more special when I know that someone has taken the time to buy a card and get it in the mail on time."

"Personally, I resent having to stop what I'm doing to pick up an e-card. Because an e-card is usually free, it also says the person didn't want to spend the money on a card. The whole thing is tacky."

"E-cards are cyberspace. They're not real. I want to touch and hold something tangible. That makes you feel good."

These comments generally echo my own feelings. I would consider sending an e-card only to a child because youngsters enjoy the technology. But I'd make sure the child is computer savvy and that someone in the household checks e-mail daily.

If you've forgotten a birthday or other occasion—and want to be perceived as a thoughtful grown-up—mail a belated note or card (which shows you made an effort), rather than send an instant e-card. An e-card gets there faster but means less. A card in the mail says you care.

That said, the rules do change, of course, if you're a shut-in or live in a rural area where it's difficult to shop for cards.

## General Tips for Electronic Communications

1. Although the salutation "Dear ————" isn't often seen in e-mails, use it to add warmth to messages and show respect for the recipient.

2. Proofread what you've written. The haste and speed of e-mail makes it all too easy to overlook errors of spelling and grammar. Such mistakes simply remind the recipient that you haven't taken the time to write thoughtfully.

3. Don't use caps, which are the equivalent of shouting.

4. Unless you don't mind coming across like a twelve-year-old, avoid emoticons, such as "smileys," to indicate tone of voice, and abbreviations such as BTW ("by the way").

5. There are levels of familiarity, and some people appreciate a certain formality of approach. Limit salutations such as "Hi, sweetie" to someone very close.

6. To make sure your e-mail flags attention and gets read, fill in the subject line with brief, focused wording, as in "Shower for Suzy." In an e-mail to a friend who had hospital tests, I used a one-word subject line: "Yesterday." Then I wrote: "How did it go at NYU Medical Center?"

7. Reread e-mails sent *to* you before replying. As you speed through your messages, it's easy to misread "can" as "cannot" or misinterpret in other ways—and to write a response that may embarrass you later.

8. Remember that e-mail can be retrieved and forwarded (intentionally or by mistake). Don't write anything you wouldn't want broadcast on the evening news.

# Part 2

## Writing Notes for Celebrations

## and Milestones

# Four

## Birthdays

When my elder son was in grade school, he sent me a card he had made by hand. It was boldly illustrated in crayon colors on cream-toned construction paper, and inside, he wrote, "Happy birthday and may all your dreams come true." I don't recall exactly which birthday I was celebrating, but I do know the words brought tears to my eyes. At that moment, all my dreams *had* come true. He had sent me a gift from the heart that was all sweetness and sincerity, unvarnished and true.

I can't think of another birthday wish that has touched me so deeply. My birthday is a time when I want to feel remembered. Once a year, that's my day. I felt my son was saying, "I love you, Mom, and I want you to be happy."

Anyone can transform a routine birthday greeting into something more meaningful by adding a personalized message to a printed card or composing an original note. To write words that matter for this once-a-year event in everyone's life, all you have to do is follow some practical pointers and ask yourself the right questions.

# Whose Birthday Is This?

Birthday greetings are an opportunity to affirm bonds with people we care about. I send personal wishes to close family members and a few dear friends. My annual birthday list includes fourteen people.

Your own list may be shorter (or longer). But, like mine, it probably does not include casual acquaintances, unless perhaps a milestone birthday is involved—or you're one of those people who just love to send cards. Some of us are especially thoughtful and do enjoy that. In general, however, you probably know the someone you're addressing very well and have definite feelings about him or her.

It's helpful to get in touch with those feelings because they will affect what you decide to say. Are you addressing someone you love . . . or like . . . or respect . . . or have mixed emotions about? Is this someone you choose to connect with—or are you writing a birthday wish out of obligation, to keep the family peace or avoid hurt feelings?

## How Does This Person Feel About the Birthday?

At the heart of a good birthday note is recognition of what that particular day means to the person. A number of variables play a role and may affect what you ultimately decide to say. One is the person's stage of life. While a six-year-old can hardly wait to be a year older, for example, few people look forward to turning forty-two . . . or fifty-four . . . or seventy.

Another issue is what is going on in the person's life at the time. An adult birthday often leads to a life review—an assessment of what has occurred in the past year (or years) and what lies ahead. That's one reason why a birthday may be stressful and why different people can feel very differently about the same birthday.

A twenty-five-year-old graduate student told me she already worries about wrinkles and notices a whole college set that is younger than she is. "All of a sudden I'm anxious about what comes next," she said. For her, the passage of time seems unwelcome. In contrast, a man I spoke to reacted to his twenty-fifth birthday with, "Hey, I've lived a quarter of a century. That's really something!"

An auto mechanic anticipates his thirty-fourth birthday, full of pride at what he's accomplished. "I messed up in school when I was a kid. I was the kind of guy who always hung out on the street and people said I'd turn out no good. Now I feel I've really built something. I've got a pretty secure job. I've raised a family and I can watch my three kids grow up," he says. A business owner the same age feels sad at his birthday and uncertain about the future. He's had a bad year. "Sales are down and the market isn't what it was. I'm wondering whether I'll have to close," he admits. "I never thought I might have to start all over at this age."

At thirty-eight, an unmarried economist glows with happiness. "For years, all I could think about was work. There was no time for much of a personal life. But I've met a wonderful new man and now we're talking about marriage and raising a family. Everything has changed," she says.

Insights like these can help stimulate meaningful associations. When writing to someone close, you may want to draw upon them.

*❋ Birthdays ❋*

Milestones are special cases, of course, and when you think about their importance, rich information emerges that you can use in what you write. Eighteen, for example, brings the promise of an unrestricted driver's license, the right to vote, college, or a job, and at twenty-one comes full adult status.

Later milestones become marker years and there are often goals people expect to have fulfilled by then. Says a travel agent, "You think you should have your life together by thirty—be married, have kids. There's pressure on you to have a career and own some property. But it's scary to still feel unsure about so much. As a woman I feel I should have a relationship by now, but I don't have that security yet. I worry that maybe I'll have to struggle by myself for my whole life." A treasured birthday message from her brother read:

*Dear* ———,

*Life takes its own sweet time. Relax and let it happen.*

*Love you on your thirtieth birthday and every day.*

Someone else recalls how depressed she felt on her thirtieth birthday. "It was 'Wake up, girl. You're getting old. The twenties are over and it's all downhill from here.'" A birthday note from her best friend told her, "Be patient. I have the feeling good things are just around the bend." The words pulled her out of the doldrums and gave her a fresh perspective. "Maybe she's right," she recalls thinking.

Forty can be experienced as a positive challenge to move on to a new phase of life—or it may be traumatic. It was for me. I realized that my life was half over and, about to embark on the second half,

I had no idea where the journey would take me. The uncertainty was frightening. I also finally understood that I was *not* going to live forever after all.

One male friend confided, "Forty was momentous. I wasn't a kid anymore. I felt I had to stop talking about what I was going to do and start producing."

Someone once told me that if you have a difficult time accepting forty, fifty will be easier (and vice versa)—that it's every other decade that shocks the psyche. For those who find fifty relatively painless, emphasis on "How am I doing?" may wane. Yet there is still awareness that time is passing.

Beginning at sixty, every five years is a milestone of sorts; sixty-five, seventy, seventy-five, and up are all special birthdays. People may be accepting of them or not, depending on issues such as health status and whether a spouse is still alive to share the celebration. Some people appreciate the wisdom and understanding that comes with age; others do not.

When you consider such issues, you can gain perspective that enriches what you write. Though you don't always know how a person feels about a birthday, often there are clues if you listen. Or, in the case of an intimate relationship, you can ask.

## WHAT DO YOU WANT TO SAY?

The whole point of a meaningful birthday note is to tell people they're special and that you care. There isn't any one set of "right words" for these sentiments, and the choices are infinite. These techniques offer a variety of ways to express what feels right to you:

## Say, "You're One of a Kind"

Is the person you're addressing a loyal and trusted friend whose wise advice has helped steer you through difficult times? Is it a sister or brother or other close relative who shares childhood memories and keeps them alive? What are the qualities you value most about the person you're writing to? People love to hear how unique they are and that they're treasured. It's a way of being validated.

Take the case of one woman who lives alone and likes it—at age ninety. Says her daughter-in-law, "She's taken up water aerobics, and afterward she sits by the pool and has lunch with a big, cackling group of friends. She just called to tell me about her new red swimsuit. She has been terrific to me, always has a sense of humor, and is happy as long as she can have chocolate bars. It takes a little more to keep me going, but when I'm ninety, I hope to be just as jovial and full of life."

I think age is a state of mind, and if this were my mother-in-law, I'd write:

*Dear ———,*

*You're younger in spirit than most people I know who are half your age—and twice as much fun. You're an inspiration and I'm lucky to have you.*

*Happy birthday.*

For the birthday of a trusted friend, I reviewed our friendship and turned to the attributes I most prized in her:

*Dear ———,*

*You're the most caring and nonjudgmental person I know.
Nobody listens like you do. You're my "sister of the soul." I
wish you a wonderful year and look forward to sharing some of
it with you.*

*Love,*

Another option is to express what's special about your relation-ship. When an aunt wished her twenty-two-year-old nephew a happy birthday, she wrote:

*Dear ———,*

*We can choose our friends, but we inherit our family. I
couldn't have handpicked a better nephew. I enjoy the fact
that we communicate so well and have become good friends.*

*Have the happiest of birthdays.*

You can also reach back for memories to say what the relation-ship means to you. A schoolteacher told me, "My aunt was central to my early life and really helped me develop my imagination. She'd go on cruises and when she returned, she'd visit and say to three-year-old me, 'Where do you want to go today?' Then she'd take me on a cruise on the couch."

For this aunt's seventy-fifth birthday, she gave back. She chose a card illustrated with a large bouquet of roses and wrote inside:

*Dear Aunt ———,*

*I want you to know how much I value your contribution in raising me. You were such an active part of my life when I was little.*

*Thanks for taking me on those adventures. I'll always remember them. Happy birthday.*

## CONSIDER WHAT IS HAPPENING

A birthday isn't an abstract idea. It's a reflection of where you are in your life, and that can be acknowledged in a message. For example, a neighbor of mine celebrated her sixtieth birthday. Though she is not my closest friend, I like her enormously. I also knew she felt unhappy about reaching this milestone. She had told me, "I hate sixty. I feel as if everything is going—my figure, my teeth, my skin. I'm falling apart."

In such situations, it's common to ignore what's real (that is, the person's negative feelings) when writing and to revert to clichés. Years ago, I would have bought a card and added, "Happy sixtieth. Congratulations and have a great day." Instead, I considered what was actually going on—her distress about aging—and took a positive approach.

This person is a wonderful woman, full of vitality, and one of the most honest people I've ever met. Such qualities are timeless. I wrote:

*Dear ———,*

*You're fresh and fun, and I can always count on you to "tell it like it is." You're a very special woman. Happy birthday.*

But a colleague said something else to a sixty-year-old who had just launched a second career as a psychologist. He wrote:

Dear ———,

*Both Freud and Marx said a happy life is love and work. At sixty, it looks to me like you've achieved both. Happy birthday.*

People also tend to appreciate wishes of good health after forty-five or so, when wellness really means something. These words are wasted, however, on young people who still feel relatively invulnerable.

What do you say to an energetic junior executive, age twenty-five, who is on his way up in the business world but anxious about not progressing on the job ladder swiftly enough? His uncle wrote:

Dear ———,

*It's not how fast you get there, it's how long you last. I have every confidence in your success. Happy birthday.*

When life is grand, you can acknowledge that:

Dear ———,

*What a great year you've had—a grant and a new baby. I hope the next one brings you more of everything you want. Happy birthday!*

Or you can personalize by referring to a specific event on the day, such as a summons to appear for jury duty. The note might read, "Happy birthday—even if you do have to spend it in court."

## Express Love, Appreciation, Admiration

Birthdays are a time for taking stock. Knowing that we have played an important role in another's life is a reason to feel good about ourselves and express caring feelings. The three words "I love you" are a powerful message and can never be anything but right when sincerely felt. You can simply add them to "Happy birthday" for a spouse or someone else dear to you. One husband gave his wife an elegant watch for her birthday to replace one she'd lost. He wrote:

*My darling:*

*You are precious to me—and, unlike any watch, irreplaceable.*

*All my love,*

When "love" doesn't fit, "I respect you" or "I admire you" might. Words like "Just to let you know I care. Have a happy, productive year" also say a great deal.

So does this note from a grateful young mother to her own mom:

*Dear Mom,*

*I appreciate the things you've done for me all year long—the books you told me to read that changed my life, the favors that took time, the nights and weekends you babysat, putting your own life "on hold."*

*I love being your daughter. Happy birthday.*

A college senior wrote to her best friend:

*Dear ——,*

*Thank you for the last four years. The experience wouldn't have been the same without you. You've enriched my life.*

*Happy birthday.*

Appreciation has broad applications, and it's appropriate to convey it to anyone who might need an extra stroke, especially the elderly. For a grandparent, you can refer to grandchildren:

*Dear ——,*

*You're a role model and it's important for you to be around the kids. They learn from you. They look up to you.*

*We love you and wish you a wonderful birthday.*

Messages like this are ideal for someone depressed or very ill, because they show that the person is valued.

Someone wrote this note to an old friend on her seventieth birthday:

*Dear ——,*

*We have so many memories together—barbecuing on the roof, the leaky motel room in Yaphank, Wendy's rained-out wedding. I can't believe you've reached this milestone and don't forget I'm right behind you.*

*No, it hasn't been a cakewalk, but you're wiser and funnier than you were then. Look around at all those who love you (including me) and don't be sad—be glad for all the new memories to come.*

*Happy birthday, dear friend.*

The writer told me that she couldn't think of anything to say that would really mean something to her friend. Then she started daydreaming about unforgettable times they'd shared. As she laughed about the memories and listed them, the affection and appreciation she felt seemed to pour out. Anytime you feel at a loss for words, focus on the person in your mind (close your eyes if it helps) and let your thoughts meander. This technique will help prompt recollections and put you in touch with your heart.

## USING HUMOR

Is your aim a light touch or a serious tone? Do you like to poke fun? Some people, especially those with a highly developed sense of humor, will chuckle at the message "Ha, ha, you're forty and I'm not" or "Happy birthday from your younger friends." But keep in mind that not everyone will.

"There's nothing funny about sixty," says one woman, who bristles at receiving humorous cards. That's why it's important to tune in to that someone you're writing to, rather than to focus on what tickles *you*.

Personally, I prefer the joke to be on both of us. A favorite line of mine, when appropriate, is "Just remember. There's always someone older than you are. Me." I also like "Bismarck said the first eighty years of a man's life are always the happiest. You've got forty to go!"

Or how about, "The upside of seventy-five is you're old enough to say anything you want and get away with it."

## SPECIAL DEVICES

There's an art to buying a card, and if you choose one that reflects the person, it adds meaning to any message inside. Are you writing an obligatory note to someone addicted to golf? Choose a card with a related illustration and add something like, "I wish you a great year on the greens. Happy birthday."

This can work for an intimate relationship, too. For the birthday of her sister, a gardener, one woman selected a card at a garden shop, featuring botanical reproductions of flowers. She then bought small sizes of some of her sister's favorite perfumes and wrote on the card:

*Dear ———,*

*I wish you a potpourri of pleasures on your birthday. Happy fortieth.*

For her brother, who worked long hours and was often stressed out, a woman slipped a gift certificate for a massage into a birthday card. She wrote: "You deserve a relaxing birthday. This will get you off to a good start. Love you a lot, brother."

*Birthdays*

One of the most imaginative birthday gifts I've heard of was the one a man gave to his father, an aeronautics engineer: a one-hour aerial tour of the locality of his choice in a single-engine plane. If I'd thought of it, I'd have written on the gift certificate: "To my father—an adventurer at any age. Happy birthday."

For the fiftieth birthday of a stockbroker, friends sent a reproduction of the front page of the *New York Times* on the day he was born. The note enclosed read:

*Dear* ———,

*We're very happy you arrived here on April 14.*

*Much love,*

Others make playful cards out of collages or drawings they've made, or create cards that are actually games. One wife's poem included clues leading to a treasure hunt for birthday gifts. She wrote:

*Because it's your birthday, [name],*
*the time is right to say,*
*that I love you more and more with each passing day.*
*And if that seems confusing,*
*please know it's meant to be.*
*It sets the mood for a game*
*I'd like you to play with me.*

*Because it's your birthday, [name],*
*and shopping's been hard to do,*

*your first surprise will be a gift.*
*Just look for the clue in your shoe.*

She proceeded to lead him with clues to the next gift.

Any card you've gone to some effort to make is a gift in itself—and of yourself. It also becomes a memento that people often keep. In such cases the card *is* the message, and "Happy Birthday . . . Love," can be enough.

You can also use interesting facts that apply. If a friend has been taking tap-dancing lessons for years, you could write to her:

*Dear ———,*

*Did you know that in 1989, Congress designated your birthday, May 25, as National Tap Dance Day? Celebrate!*

When you're stuck, you can always tie in information about the person's birthstone. If your spouse was born in April, how about something like:

*Dear ———,*

*Your birthstone is a diamond, rare, known for its brilliance, and precious. How appropriate.*

*Have a happy birthday.*

*All my love,*

## BELATED BIRTHDAYS

A close friend wrote to me:

> *Dear Florence,*
>
> *Just want to thank you for your birthday note. You always remember. You're so good at these things and I'm not. So I wish you a happy birthday for all those times I forgot.*

I appreciated her words, but little does she know about the times birthdays have slipped by me. When I do forget, my rule of thumb is that it's never too late to send good wishes. Most people understand, but honesty is essential.

Here's a belated note I've written (with variations) to a number of people:

> *Dear ———,*
>
> *Your birthday is carefully penciled in on my calendar. The trouble is, I forgot to look at the calendar.*
>
> *I'm sorry for sending these wishes late, but they come from the heart. Have a wonderful year ahead.*

Another option is:

> *Dear ———,*
>
> *The best of intentions run amok. I fully intended to wish you a happy birthday and want you to know I'm thinking of you now. Hope your [number] birthday was a memorable one.*

When I've forgotten a birthday, I much prefer to send (and receive) a sincere note or personalized greeting card, rather than an instant e-card. On the other hand, e-mail is a great way to follow up a birthday card to someone important to you. A message like, "How did you celebrate your big day? Want to hear all about it," is an excuse to connect and share.

## BIRTHDAY NOTES FOR CHILDREN

It's hard to imagine an event more important to a child than a birthday. Receiving a personalized birthday message is a significant experience as well, because people rarely write to children, and children usually don't correspond with one another. Most of the mail that comes to the home is for grown-ups. When youngsters do receive something addressed to them, it makes them feel important and respected—they remember it.

Here's how to write a meaningful message to the children in your life.

### 1. TRY FOR TRUTH AND BE SENSITIVE.

Never write anything that sounds pretentious, makes fun of children, or demeans or embarrasses them. Skip the saccharine sentiments and lines like, "To my dearest, darling ———," unless you really feel them. Remember, too, that most children don't like corn.

What children do want to hear is that they're special and cared about. Whether you're writing a note to a niece or nephew, grandchild, neighbor, or friend, show that you know who the child is. Be specific and indicate why you love (or feel affection for) this particular youngster, as in, "You're my oldest niece and you're always number one to me." This is a way of explaining your relationship to a child—and it can mean a great deal.

## 2. SEND SOMETHING AGE-APPROPRIATE.

For very young children, it's the object (the card itself) that makes an impact, rather than the message. Choose (or make) cards that are visually appealing, contain an element of surprise, and/or involve an activity, such as pop-up cards and cards that contain games or pictures that can be colored in.

Kiss a card. Apply heavy red lipstick, then imprint your lips. Underneath you can write, "Love and kisses from ———." The message can be read to children who are too young to read for themselves.

Another graphic gimmick: when you sign off with "Love from ———," try making a "smiley face" or a heart out of the first *o*.

For older children, draw a birthday cake with flaming candles and paste a dime on each flame. A seven-year-old gets seven dimes. Children also love quarters taped all over the inside of a card.

Make a card for an older child in the style of a ransom note, cutting letters out of magazines and newspapers in different sizes, colors, and typefaces to form the words HAPPY BIRTHDAY.

Coupons work well, too, and lend themselves to personalization. One dad made his own card for his son's birthday, illustrating it with drawings of various kinds of sushi, the boy's favorite food. He wrote on it, "Redeemable for one sushi dinner at a restaurant you choose. Valid till [date]."

## 3. KEY IN TO INTERESTS.

Children develop passions as early as the toddler years. For one preschooler who was mesmerized by garbage trucks, family members sent birthday cards with notes like, "To the cutest garbageman we know."

Six-year-old girls may collect dolls and items from nature; elementary-school boys often build rock collections. One grandmother included a note with her gift:

*Dear ———,*

*Happy birthday to my gem of a grandson. I think I've found a specimen for your rock collection.*

She printed the message, since children in the early grades usually can't read script.

To a child into sports, try "Happy birthday to my favorite third baseman" for a Little Leaguer, or "I hear you're the newest member of the soccer team."

When writing to a teen, focus on what's important to the youngster. Has your niece become very fashion conscious? You might say:

*Dear ———,*

*How lucky I am to have such a bright and stylish niece. I love the new haircut. Happy birthday.*

*Love,*

Beware of intruding when writing to adolescents, however, and avoid questions about social life. Today, some thirteen-year-olds go steady, while others don't date at all. Even those who do date resent adults asking about boyfriends and girlfriends, say experts. Also avoid questions about grades. If you know the child has achieved something, however, you *can* say, "Your parents told me how well you're doing in school and I'm so happy to hear that."

4. ASK YOURSELF IF SOMETHING SPECIAL HAPPENED TO THIS CHILD IN THE PAST YEAR.

Religious school or music lessons often start at nine or ten. How about:

*Dear ——,*

*Mom tells me you've joined the marching band. That's great. Have a terrific birthday.*

*Love,*

Is a teen getting ready to drive? I'd write:

*Dear ——,*

*This is going to be a great year. I'm so glad that you're taking driver's ed. Happy birthday.*

Talk about a child's accomplishments, as in, "How wonderful that your picture was chosen for the school art show," (or, "that you've learned to ride a two-wheeler"). It's a nongender approach and validates that something important is going on.

If your fifteen-year-old nephew became assistant editor of his high school newspaper, you could write:

*Dear ———,*

*I know how hard you're working at the paper and I was very impressed with the article your mom showed me. I'm proud to have a newsman in the family. Happy birthday.*

## 5. DON'T FORGET YOUR OWN CHILD.

Many parents don't write birthday notes to sons and daughters. Yet youngsters want your approval, and this is an opportunity to express your love and forge intimacy. Now that my own sons are older, I still take this chance to tell them, in writing, how much they mean to me.

There's a difference between looking forward to being a year older and looking forward to notes that show others care. At nineteen or ninety, people have one thing in common: they do want to be remembered. Since your words mean so much, it's worth taking the time to write a more meaningful message.

# Five

## Anniversaries

*Twenty years is a long time. It's a real badge of honor, with all the marriages I've seen breaking up. I'm proud of my husband and myself.*

*Ours is definitely a love match, so our anniversary is the most special day on the calendar. The kids know that, too. They're fully prepared for Mom and Dad going goo-goo over each other.*

*An anniversary is a transition, a time to review our relationship and ask, What can we do to make it better?*

A wedding anniversary is a celebration of a relationship and of reaching a point in life's journey together. Because it's a very personal, private event between two people, couples don't usually expect others to mark the occasion. Yet each year, you probably remember the anniversaries of a few couples who are important to you—perhaps those of immediate family and/or close friends whose wedding you attended. The list may expand when acknowledging milestones like a twenty-fifth, fiftieth, or even sixtieth anniversary.

How can you acknowledge these events (and your own anniversary, as well) by writing something personal and meaningful? That can depend on the couple and certain other variables. When you take them into account, it's easier than you realize to say "Happy anniversary" in a special and individualized way.

## WRITING TO FAMILY OR FRIENDS

The purpose of an anniversary message is to honor a marriage and, usually, to tell two people they're important to you. To unlock the flow of words, it helps to consider such issues as which anniversary is being celebrated, the tone of the marriage, whether it's a first or second (or third) marriage, and your own sincere feelings.

Here's how to find the right words:

### 1. GIVE A GLIMPSE OF HOW THE MARRIAGE LOOKS TO OTHERS.

All couples want to hear that their relationship is special. Why not mention the qualities you see and most admire in their marriage?

For example, old friends of mine are a dual-career couple. They're two people who are truly interested in each other's (very different) work, are dedicated parents of three children, and share passionate interests in hiking, horseback riding, and other outdoor activities. To mark their anniversary, I might write:

*Dear ——— and ———,*

*Indoors or out, you look awfully good to me. The respect and support you share shows that the smartest thing you ever did was marry each other.*

*Happy anniversary.*

*Love,*

On the other hand, I'd write something very different to another couple. When they walked down the aisle, people said it wouldn't last. The bride was not only eight years older than the groom, she already had two children from a previous marriage. But they beat the odds. They adore each other, have had a baby together, and he's a caring father to all three children. This couple has built a strong marriage in very difficult circumstances, and validation of what they've achieved has meaning in an anniversary message.

Second marriages have a harder time of it than first marriages. The divorce rate is higher. Life is far more complicated when families are blended and partners must take on relationships with stepchildren. Couples are likely to appreciate acknowledgment of their special situation through words like:

*Dear ——— and ———,*

*What a great team you are. Marriage isn't easy, but you've made it look that way and built a wonderful family. You're a special pair. Here's to many more good years ahead.*

*Happy anniversary.*

Though marriage can be taken for granted as the years go by, there are some couples wed twenty, thirty, or even forty years who still look at each other like newlyweds. These relationships aren't necessarily any better than anyone else's, say experts, but the partners are demonstrative and they work at keeping the spark between them alive.

Capture the essence of such a duo with words like:

*Dear ——— and ———,*

*I remember last New Year's Eve, when you got up to dance. You looked like starry-eyed prom dates. You've got the secret formula for keeping romance alive. Bottle it!*

## 2. MENTION THE WEDDING, IF YOU ATTENDED.

You tend to feel a special connection to a couple if you were present at the nuptials. It's helpful to reminisce about the day and try to recall details that bring a smile. Sharing memories is a way to acknowledge the bond you feel.

One woman wrote to her sister and brother-in-law:

*Dear ——— and ———,*

*I remember standing beside you in the judge's chambers and how happy you looked. You still look that way (most of the time).*

*Love you both. Happy anniversary.*

### 3. FOCUS ON YOUR RELATIONSHIP WITH THEM.

An anniversary note is a way to maintain family ties and affirm bonds of friendship. Ask, "Why do I value these two people?"

I wrote to an aunt and uncle:

*Dear ———— and ————,*

*You've always been like second parents. You've shared the happy moments in my life, and the sad, and I appreciate your love. You're very dear to me.*

*Happy anniversary.*

### 4. LOOK AT WHAT'S HAPPENED RECENTLY.

Did the couple have a new baby, move to a new apartment, buy a house, take new jobs, retire? Try:

*Dear ———— and ————,*

*Your beautiful new twins make this an anniversary to remember. May this be just the beginning of many happy years ahead.*

### 5. HONOR MILESTONES.

People often take a special trip for a milestone anniversary, and you can mention that. Or express congratulations, something like:

*Dear ———— and ————,*

*Two decades is quite an achievement and you have a right to feel proud. Celebrate in style. You've earned it!*

*Happy anniversary.*

For a fortieth, fiftieth, or sixtieth anniversary, "What an accomplishment" is always right. Any couple married this long has experienced plenty of ups and downs and is worthy of admiration. You can add (assuming it's true), "You've built a wonderful life together." But do personalize by mentioning a specific detail or two, such as grandchildren.

At the very least, mention the anniversary number, even if you have to settle for a benign message like "Congratulations on reaching the silver twenty-five." Unlike birthdays, anniversaries are usually welcomed as the numbers mount.

Many people today (including some senior citizens) have long-term committed relationships but are not married. A note or card that congratulates them on a milestone of ten or twenty years (or more) together recognizes the importance and permanence of the relationship. It's likely to be appreciated precisely because such acknowledgments are rare. I wrote this message to close friends:

*Dear ——— and ———,*

*You're the most compatible couple I know. Getting together was the best thing you ever did. Happy 25th anniversary.*

*Love,*

## WRITING TO YOUR SPOUSE

"Our anniversary is an opportunity to tell you that I love you," wrote one husband—and so it is. It's the perfect time to stop, reflect on your relationship, and write a caring reminder of the commitment you've made to each other. Here are ways to help you express loving sentiments at your house:

## 1. RECALL HOW YOU MET.

My husband and I met in an elevator. He was the handsome stranger wearing the uniform of a U.S. Navy lieutenant, and I thought he looked vaguely familiar. In fact, he lived in the apartment above mine while assigned to a local recruiting station. Two years later, we married, and what bound us together was not only our initial attraction, but the dreams and goals for the future that we shared. Some have been realized, others not. We've experienced the difficult times and disappointments that come with the territory in any marriage, no matter how happy. In a way, they make our wedding anniversary even sweeter.

To mark the day last year, I bought an anniversary card for my husband and added:

*Dear ———,*

*The minute I saw you in that elevator, I knew you were the man for me. You still are.*

*I love you more than ever. Happy anniversary.*

The words didn't trip off my tongue. As I sat down to write, I happened to think of our first encounter. A flood of warm memories followed that seemed to renew the significance of our anniversary and led to the expression of loving thoughts.

Without realizing it, I'd stumbled upon an approach similar to one used by some marriage therapists. They ask spouses to remember in detail the circumstances of their first meeting, to recall first impressions and exactly what it was that attracted one to the other. It's a way to get in touch with a bank of happy memories.

## 2. PULL OUT YOUR WEDDING ALBUM.

One husband leafs through the pages each year and finds that the familiar photographs cause all kinds of associations and happy memories to spill out. He recently wrote to his wife:

*Dear ———,*

*The day we got married was the best day of my life. I felt so happy. After eleven years, I still do.*

*Happy anniversary, my love.*

## 3. SHOW APPRECIATION.

One way to do this is to mention the qualities you love in your spouse:

*Dear ———,*

*I love you because you make me laugh . . . because you surprise me . . . because you're my best friend. What would I do without you?*

*Happy anniversary.*

One husband recounted what he felt on his fifth anniversary: "I sat in the living room while my wife and son were sleeping, and I thought of my life before marriage and of what the future would be like without my family. I concluded I really like my life now and I'm content. But that would not be so if I didn't have my wife." He wrote to her:

*Dear* ———,

*You've made me a happy man. I'm yours always—today, tomorrow, and forever.*

*Happy anniversary.*

On their fortieth anniversary, a wife wrote:

*My dearest honey,*

*I can't believe it's forty years, but what a grand time it's been. No one else could have made my life as fulfilling and exciting.*

*I love you now and forever. So what do you have in mind for our forty-fifth?*

*All my kisses,*

4. ACKNOWLEDGE THE GOOD AND THE BAD.

Life can be tough and full of ups and downs. If you and your mate have had a difficult year, acknowledging that fact can help bring you closer together. One couple experienced a year marked by family illness and financial disappointments. For their eighteenth anniversary, the wife acknowledged the circumstances in her own loving way and wrote: "We've made it together through thick and thin. I'll always love you."

Another eloquent note read:

*Dear ———,*

*How did we survive you losing your job, me losing my father, and two robberies—all in the last twelve months? We're a great team, and always have been.*

*I love you more than ever. Happy anniversary.*

---

## BELATED ANNIVERSARIES

It's just as easy to forget an anniversary as a birthday. I felt embarrassed when I discovered I'd failed to acknowledge the milestone anniversary of dear friends. I wrote this note:

*Dear ——— and ———,*

*We're mortified that we "slept" right past your fortieth. That's a milestone to shout about. Belatedly, we wish you the happiest of anniversaries. You've both chosen well.*

*To many more good years ahead.*

---

Many spouses say, "My anniversary means a lot to me." But others, especially some wed many years, are surprisingly unsentimental, describing an anniversary as "just another day, though we go out to dinner."

Yet it can be so much more than that. When you write loving words to your spouse, it is a gift; but it is also a gift to yourself that can help recharge deep feelings and confirm your bond.

*Anniversaries*

$Six$

# Weddings and Engagements

*We've been living together for a year, so people tend to say, "What's different about marriage?" But I'm looking forward to starting a family and a life with someone. The ritual—the public acknowledgment of the commitment—makes it more real for me. Saying, "This is my boyfriend" doesn't suggest that this is a permanent relationship or reflect my depth of feeling about it.*

*Our wedding meant so much because it was a second marriage for both of us. We'd been burned once and it meant we were taking another chance. I felt very confident that this was going to work and so grateful that I found this wonderful person. I appreciated how rare it is to find a real helpmate.*

*Sharing my future with the person I care most about is the biggest decision and the biggest commitment I've ever made.*

A happy ending, a new beginning, a life together . . . that's what weddings are all about. And what you communicate in a card or note of congratulations (with or without a gift) can set the tone for decades to come. A meaningful message says, "I know how important this event is in your life. It matters to me and it makes me joyful for you."

It isn't always easy to convey these feelings in a natural and personal way. It takes some thought to move beyond clichés. Yet when you realize how much a wedding means to a couple (and the whole family), isn't it worth your time?

Here's how to avoid sounding as if this is just another obligation you have to deal with and instead write a message that says, "I care."

## WHO'S GETTING MARRIED?

The whole reason for writing is to celebrate a couple on what is clearly their most special of days and to express your pleasure about it. What you say and how you say it, however, will be affected by your relationship with the bride and groom. If either is a close friend or relative, this is the time for intimacy and words of love and affection. On the other hand, you can't—and shouldn't try to—write an intimate note to someone you don't know well.

## HOW DO YOU FEEL ABOUT IT?

Weddings involve powerful combinations of joy, anticipation, hopes, fears, anxieties, expectations. Guests and other well-wishers feel a range of emotions, too. When you dig a little deeper to get in touch with your own feelings, the results may surprise you.

Sometimes you may need to deal with negative emotions, such as your conviction that your sister is marrying someone all wrong for her. Or you may feel ambivalent about how marriage will change your relationship with a close friend. You want to accent the positive, but you *can* take your feelings into account to write something honest that is also appropriate.

## WHAT DO YOU WANT TO SAY?

A meaningful note sounds sincere and true, not trite, and honors a particular couple on this particular wedding day.

Here are some strategies for finding the right words:

### 1. REFLECT ON THE COUPLE.

If you're close, this is the perfect time to think about your relationship with the bride and groom and why they (and the wedding) are important to you. You can recap memories and express your support. One bride, who loved the note she received from her closest friend, told me, "She wrote about how central we are in her life and how valuable. She mentioned three things we've been through together, including a series of her boyfriends." The note closed with, "I'm so lucky to have such loyal and trusted friends. You deserve the best and you're both getting it. Love, ———"

You can also comment on how their relationship looks to you. Is it a real love match? A groom's friend wrote, "I think there are very few people in the world who *should* be married. You are two of them." He talked about all the positive changes the bride had brought to the groom's life and concluded with, "I've never seen [name of groom] happier or two people who belonged together as much as you do. That makes *me* happy. This is one wedding I look forward to."

A sister-in-law wrote

*Dear ———,*

*Some people get married because time is marching and "it's time to settle down." But it was clear from the very beginning that you were truly meant for each other. I'm thrilled to see you walking down the aisle.*

This note echoed parents' wishes:

*Dear ———,*

*Your mother wanted someone for you who loves, understands, and admires you and is a true partner for your journey through this very difficult life. She told me that you and [name of groom] are soul mates and how happy she is that you are so well matched. I'm delighted, too.*

*All my love,*

Is this a second marriage where the bride and groom endured many tough years of loneliness before meeting? Do you feel moved? Then say something like, "Thank goodness you found each other! Nobody deserves happiness more than you do and I feel teary eyed when I think of your big day."

## 2. WELCOME THE NEW SPOUSE.

A wedding is a life-cycle event that brings a new partner into the circle of family. You can celebrate that entrance and comment on the person's positive qualities: "Joe is so funny and smart. I love him already. How fortunate we are to have him join our family."

A groom's relative wrote to a bride,

*Dear ———,*

*What a wonderful choice [name of groom] has made. Welcome to the family.*

And what a wonderful way to cement family relations.

Often, in a second marriage, two family units are being forged into one. If the bride or groom has children, you may want to mention them in a welcoming way, as in, "How nice it will be to see the children at the wedding."

3. REFER TO CONTINUITY OF THE GENERATIONS.

This note refers to the continuity symbolized by a marriage:

*Dear ———,*

*I've known your parents for thirty years. I attended their wedding and I remember the day you were born. Your father was so excited and moved, he burst into tears.*

*Now, as I see you taking this important next step in life, I'm honored and proud to share your wedding day.*

You can also tie the generations together with a message of inclusion: "Your father always played piano and it's wonderful to know that [name of groom] is also talented on the keyboard. I can see that Mozart will be heard in your home, just as it was when you were growing up."

Or try, "We've never had a doctor in the family. It's about time!"

4. Acknowledge the preparations.

One bride told me, "The wedding was such an exciting buildup. We'd planned it for so long and six or seven months of our lives revolved around it. We met with photographers, caterers, florists, musicians. It wasn't until the end that all the pieces fit into place. I was amazed it went so well."

The couple and their families are trying to please you, and you may want to acknowledge their effort in your note. If your gift is sent after the wedding (as many are), you'll know (and can talk about) the details firsthand. When writing before the event, you might handle it this way:

*Dear ——— and ———,*

*I know how much planning went into this day. Your mother told me how many hotels you looked at, the care you took with the menu, and how you both designed the invitations.*

*I feel privileged to attend such a special wedding.*

You can also comment on a unique feature of the wedding, such as the view or location. Is it a "funky" affair, held on a river pier? Try, "I've been invited to lots of weddings, but yours is one of a kind. It sounds like great fun. Looking forward."

Destination weddings have become very popular. If you're invited to nuptials in Las Vegas, couples' number-one destination choice, you might write:

*Dear ——— and ———,*

*Congratulations to both of you. You picked my favorite place for your wedding. I'll be there to help you celebrate.*

Or try:

*Dear ——— and ———,*

*I'm smiling as I anticipate your walking down the aisle in Cancún. What a terrific locale for your wedding.*

*Congratulations.*

Will there be a special kind of ceremony? Say something like, "I've never been to a military wedding before. I can't imagine anything more romantic. Can't wait!"

5. PERSONALIZE WITH OTHER DEVICES.

You can always tie your words in to the gift you give. A financial analyst sent a Pueblo wedding vase to close friends. In his note, he discussed the symbolism of the ceramic vessel—that two separate people have now become one family—and quoted the chant associated with it.

Or focus on a personal detail. If the couple has lived together, and you know them well, comment on their habits or lifestyle. One friend wrote to wacky pack rats:

*Dear ——— and ———,*

*There's no doubt you're made for each other. With your collections of paperweights, posters, and whatever, the only question is, when will you burst out of your apartment?*

*I love you both and feel absolutely thrilled you're getting married.*

On one occasion, I wrote to a couple I barely knew (my connection was through the parents), and I couldn't think of a thing to say. My solution was to mention the wedding date:

*Dear ——— and ———,*

*We're so honored to share this special time with you. We'll always remember June 25 as your wedding day. We wish you a life of love and a happy home.*

## 6. LIMIT ADVICE.

Give it only if it means something and represents wisdom gleaned from your own experience. I like what a young wife wrote to her friends: "Be good to each other and let your lives and love grow. This is only the beginning."

Many of the preceding examples can be used for gay and lesbian ceremonies. Another option is to talk about what the word *commitment* signifies: "Commitment means giving in trust and pledging oneself. We're delighted to celebrate your commitment to each other. Congratulations on your big day."

A businessman wrote to his younger sister and her partner:

*Dear ——— and ———,*

*There's no doubt about the state of your union. You make each other so happy. May you share a life of love always.*

When her nephew and his partner wed in Canada, one woman expressed her good wishes this way: "Your marriage is a sign of your great love for one another. I wish you every happiness."

---

### Responses to Wedding Invitations

Whether you reply with your own separate note, which is most correct, or fill in a printed response card, it's nice to convey enthusiasm, caring, love, affection—all the good things we need from each other. Families appreciate cards that say "will *be delighted to* attend" or "will attend *with pleasure*."

Or you can add an extra, personal line to the response card. One mother of the bride told me, "I used to run home to read these responses and I'd call my husband at the office or my daughter to share them." Here are some I like:

*We can't wait.*

*I want to come!*

*You bet.*

*Of course we'll attend.*

---

*As if there's any chance we'd miss it.*

*Count us in.*

*We accept with pleasure your invitation to the wedding of your daughter to* one lucky guy!

Incidentally, if you can't attend, it's nice to imply that you wish you could have, as in, "We're so sorry we'll have to miss what we know will be a beautiful wedding. Although we can't be there, we'll be thinking of [names of bride and groom] and celebrating in our hearts."

Even better is a note that includes a cogent reason for not coming, as in, "I would love to attend, but I will be on my way to Australia. Know that I'll be there in spirit."

Respond to an invitation promptly—within seven to ten days of receipt, unless the RSVP card indicates a longer reply deadline. Reply early especially if you cannot attend to allow the couple enough time to invite someone else if they wish. Do not respond to a formal wedding invitation via e-mail.

## WRITING TO PARENTS OF THE COUPLE

I recently attended a beautiful spring wedding held outdoors in the country. It brought together three generations of a devoted family, and I wrote to the parents the next day:

*Dear —— and ——,*

*It was truly a joy to share [names of bride and groom]'s wedding day. They both looked so happy, and how lucky they are to have a family like you.*

Another option is something like:

*Dear ——,*

*My thanks for allowing me to share such a beautiful day on Sunday. The wedding was delightful and [names of bride and groom] are a charming couple.*

*Every detail was perfect from where I sat.*

*Many congratulations.*

## ENGAGEMENTS

An engagement, which lasts an average of sixteen months in the United States, is the start of a whirlwind period. Congratulations make a special impression. One young woman appreciated this note from a close family friend:

*Dear ——,*

*What wonderful news. Your mom tells me that the relationship with [name of fiancé] is a deep love affair.*

*Accept my love and congratulations and give [name of fiancé] a big hug for me, too. When you decide on some of the objects you want in your home, let me know so I can buy something for you and be present all the time in your lives.*

Along with a gift of a wedding planner came these words: "The most exciting and frantic time of your life is about to begin. Since you told me you want this wedding to be perfect, hope this helps." Another option:

*Dear ———,*

*We remember you as that bright, smiling little girl back in third grade. It's a joy to know what a wonderful woman you've become. We're so happy to hear about your engagement and plan to come to cheer you on at your wedding.*

An aunt wrote to her nephew:

*Dear ———,*

*I want to be first on line to congratulate you on your engagement. You always said you'd get married at thirty. You're a year ahead of schedule.*

*I've heard all about [fiancée's name] and look forward to meeting her. (Does she know what a catch she's getting?)*

*All my love and good wishes,*

By all means e-mail if you want to capture the immediacy of this occasion, as in, "Dear ———, So she finally said yes. Hooray." Understand, however, that this does not replace a congratulatory note or card for the engagement.

E-mail works, too, when the person who has become engaged is merely an acquaintance—for example, the secretary of a business contact. You've met her in person once, although you've e-mailed and talked on the phone. You probably wouldn't send a card, but you might dash off an e-mail saying something like, "Dear ———, I heard about your engagement. Wonderful news. Congratulations." She's likely to smile and think, "What a nice thing to do," and go out of her way for you in the future.

A marriage is one of our most intense and hopeful life experiences. It makes couples and their families happy to receive all those cards and notes and know people are excited for them. Writing good wishes can reward you, too.

# Seven

## Births, Adoptions, Pregnancy

After several frustrating trips abroad and much anxiety, angst, and red tape, a couple I know finally arranged to adopt a baby girl from South America. They had overcome many obstacles in making this adoption a reality and I admired their courage. It was an on-again, off-again affair that stretched the limits of patience and determination, but when their infant daughter finally arrived, it was cause for celebration. I sent a gift for the baby and wrote on the enclosed card:

*Dear [name of baby],*

*Welcome to the United States! You certainly picked the right family. I can't wait to meet you.*

*Love,*

The arrival of a new baby is a joy and a miracle, whatever the circumstances, and a birth or adoption deserves a message echoing the happiness and hope everyone feels. Whether you're writing a card or note to close friends or family, distant relatives, or a professional acquaintance, here's how to mark one of the most precious moments in life and say something that will be remembered long after the bottles and diapers are packed away.

## GUIDELINES FOR NOTES

The purpose of writing is to congratulate parents (and/or grandparents and possibly great-grandparents), celebrate a child, and welcome a new family member—in a way that is specific to the people involved. In many cases, you'll find inspiration fast when you focus on a few key questions: What is special about this baby? What is unique about the situation? How do you feel about it? Then try one of these strategies:

### 1. ACKNOWLEDGE WHAT A SPECIAL TIME THIS IS.

The birth of a baby is a universally cosmic experience. As one new father put it, "When I saw my son, I can only describe my feeling as sublime happiness. From then on, life became more fulfilling."

A family is touched and changed by a baby. One grandmother was so overjoyed when her daughter had twins that she sat down and wrote to her: "You have given me such a precious gift. Thank you for letting me be a part of these babies' lives." Is it any wonder she and her daughter have a close, loving relationship?

But even if your relationship is not intimate, you can still communicate, "I know this is an important time." When I sent a baby gift to a couple I'd met only a few times, I wrote this accompanying note:

*Dear ——— and ———,*

*We're delighted to welcome [name of baby] into the family. Your mom has promised to bring plenty of pictures when she visits next week, so we can see [name of baby] for ourselves. Congratulations!*

When a dental hygienist became a new mother, she received a gift from a longtime patient, along with this note:

*Dear ———,*

*I'm just so happy for you guys. Take care of yourself, along with your new son. This is a time to cherish. Spend lots of it with [name of baby] and enjoy him.*

If you know it (or can find it out), a mention of the baby's name instantly adds a personal element. When addressing the mother, rather than both parents, you may also want to make some reference to Dad in what you write.

To congratulate the older generation, try something like, "What wonderful news that you're grandparents again. I'm so happy to hear [name of daughter or daughter-in-law] had a baby girl. May [name of baby] bring you love and joy."

## 2. FACTOR IN WHAT'S UNIQUE ABOUT THE CHILD.

Is it a first baby? Or a first boy or girl? (Or a second girl, just like you?) Is it your first niece or nephew (or the first in a long time)? Are you genuinely excited? There's always *something* you can find to write about—and it can trigger other warm associations.

*Births, Adoptions, Pregnancy*

Let's say your cousin had a first girl after two boys. You might write something like, "How wonderful that you're finally enjoying the experience of a little girl. I'm thrilled that you now have a daughter." Beware, however, of statements like "You finally got your boy [or girl]." They place a value on the gender of the child and sound sexist—and the parents may not feel the way you do.

"I just wanted a healthy baby. It wasn't important what sex it was," says one mom. Another who had a third girl told me, "I didn't want a boy. I'm good at girls. I wasn't in the mood to learn something new. There's something rich about the household when the children are all females or all males."

Look for something else that's special. Did the baby arrive in December? Try something like:

*Dear ——— and ———,*

*This year there's really something to celebrate. What a splendid Christmas present [name of baby] is to the whole family.*

If the lineup at home is all boys, I like this message: "Hugs and kisses and a big warm hello to [name of baby]. Ah, boys. Love and laundry!"

## 3. CONSIDER THE SITUATION.

Anytime there's a long, hard struggle involved in becoming a parent, there's an extra measure of joy when the moment finally arrives. Well-wishers also feel moved when the odds are overcome, and you can warm up what you write by expressing such feelings.

For example, I wanted to cheer when a couple I know finally succeeded in having a baby through in vitro fertilization, as I said in my note:

*Dear ———— and ————,*

*I'm so thrilled for you that I feel like cheering. Hooray for [name of baby]!*

*Lots of love,*

One woman who had a first baby at forty, after overcoming medical problems, told me, "The birth of my son was a triumph." I might echo her own words and write, "[Name of baby] is a triumph and a very special blessing. I wish you joy—and more joy."

You can also celebrate the parents, if you know them well. When her sister-in-law finally gave birth after three miscarriages, one woman wrote, "What a wonderful mom you'll be. I can't think of anyone more nurturing than you are. How lucky [name of baby] is to have you as a parent."

Of course, special circumstances don't always involve adversity. When a couple with adolescent children decided to have a very wanted baby, a friend thought about the excitement that would accompany going back to this stage of life by choice. She wrote:

*Dear ———— and ————,*

*How wonderful it is that you're new parents again. I feel so excited for you. [Name of baby] is going to keep you both young!*

### 4. Be sensitive to adoptions.

Just like a birth, an adoption is a once-in-a-lifetime experience—and a *very* happy occasion. But do keep the differences in mind when you choose to jot your note on a greeting card. Some cards are clearly intended for births (such as those with lines like "Congratulations on the birth of your son") and will only serve as reminders of what did *not* happen.

When expressing personal good wishes, be aware of the words you choose and remember that, often, less is more. In general, it's wise to avoid mentioning "adoption" (and cards that do so). Instead, you can take your cue from the announcement for an adopted child, which will usually say, "[Name of baby] has arrived" or "[Name of baby] has joined the family." Use the same terminology when you write, as in, "We're so happy James has joined the family." Or you can try, "We're thrilled that Megan is here at last," without going into detail.

If you know the parents intimately and wish to acknowledge the emotional roller coaster of the adoption process, you might add, "I know how hard you worked to make this happen." Or, "I know how wanted this baby is and how special."

### 5. Mention siblings.

Parents appreciate notes that remember older children, as in, "We're so happy to welcome a brother for Annie and John into the family." Or, "How wonderful Annie and John have a new sister." But beware of something like "Annie and John must be so thrilled to have a brother," unless you know it's true. My own son's reaction when I brought his baby brother home from the hospital was, "What do we need *him* for!"

## 6. REFER TO THE BIRTH ANNOUNCEMENT.

If a picture of the baby accompanied the announcement, you might comment (when appropriate), "What a beautiful baby [name of baby] is." Every parent wants to hear words like that. If the baby isn't adorable, you can try something like, "You must be so proud of [name of baby]."

You can also tie your message in to the child's name, as in, "[Name of baby] is such a beautiful name. It's my grandmother's name and I've always loved it."

Or try something along the lines of:

*Dear ——— and ———,*

*It's wonderful to know the family tree continues to grow. [Name of baby] brings fresh life and hope to us all. Congratulations and much love.*

Was the birth announcement a blueprint, including the baby's specifications? I'd write something like, "[Name of baby] undoubtedly has a great future ahead. Look at the architects!"

## 7. TRY OTHER DEVICES.

Since a note often comes with a gift, you can key in your message to the item. Aware that a colleague had difficulty getting her new baby to sleep, one woman sent a lullaby tape as a gift, along with a note reading, "This got my son to close his eyes. I hope it helps you with Henry as much as it helped me." Or try, "My baby loved this crib toy. It really kept him busy. Hope Robert will like it, too."

Practical advice can be comforting when it comes from people who are relaxed about their own children. Says the mother of two preschoolers, "I was drained from lack of sleep as a new mom and was terrified it would never end. So I tell first-time parents in my notes, 'You *will* sleep again. It only lasts a few months. Then you can be awake and really enjoy [name of baby].'"

Or you might want to take the creative route. Says a recent mom, "I always walk around the office with a pencil in my mouth. When I gave birth, a coworker made a card for me. He drew a cartoon of a baby with a pencil in its mouth and wrote, 'To Jennifer. Just like Mom.' Of course I kept it in my album!"

This is a time when a new mother's hormones are running wild and she's likely to find even the simplest words touching. Parents who have adopted are in a state of euphoria as well.

Don't forget grandparents. They're excited about the baby too. Write or e-mail something like, "Congratulations on your new grandchild. How lucky [name of baby] is to have you in his [or her] life." Or try, "Best wishes on becoming a grandparent again. [Name of child] gives us all hope for the future."

## BABIES WITH DIFFICULTIES

Sometimes an infant is born with Down's syndrome or some other major health problem. In these cases, we often don't know what to say. What can you write? First, try to get a reading on how the parents feel about what has happened. Some parents look upon such a birth as a challenge. In this case, if you're close, you can acknowledge the family's strength and love, as in, "This baby is coming into a wonderful family." Or, "How fortunate that [name of baby] will be part of your warm, caring family. Remember, our friendship and love are here for you." If the parents have shared their fears with you, you might say something comforting and positive, such as, "This family has much to give to a child with special challenges."

On the other hand, the toughest time to write is when parents feel that they are being punished. Here you might talk in terms of, "I'm thinking of you and how you are managing."

In general, keep the message short and simple. If you don't know the parents' reaction, acknowledge this birth like any other birth—without getting effusive about it, as in, "Congratulations on the birth of your new son [or daughter]." You can add an expression of caring, such as, "We send our love to you and [name of baby]."

What do you write in a tentative situation, as when a very premature baby may not survive? You might combine support with congratulations as in, "Congratulations on your little girl. We're rooting for [name of baby]." If you want to offer help, suggest something specific, such as babysitting an older child while the parents are at the hospital.

Writing on the occasion of a difficult birth may feel awkward, but parents in such situations need more than ever to know that their friends are concerned and there for them. A note that recognizes the struggle and lends support can be invaluable to people facing such challenges.

## PREGNANCY

If you know someone is happy to be expecting, you share in the joyous anticipation when you acknowledge what has happened. Your note is likely to be remembered, too, because it may be the only one received at this time. Pregnancy usually isn't considered an occasion to write in the way a birth is.

I sent this note to a friend's daughter who had been trying to have a baby:

*Dear ———,*

*We're thrilled to hear you're going to be a mommy! Bill must be ecstatic, along with your parents. Take good care of yourself.*

*All the best,*

This e-mail congratulated soon-to-be grandparents, who announced in their Christmas letter that their daughter was pregnant: "What great news that Pat is due in May. You're going to be the best grandparents. We're so happy for you."

Everyone's emotional when a new baby arrives—parents *and* grandparents. When you write something that shares the joy, your note will bring pleasure to any family.

# Eight

## Rites of Passage

### First Communions, Confirmations, Bar and Bat Mitzvahs, La Quinceañera, Graduations

Each of the following events represents a major turning point in someone's (usually a youngster's) life. What can you write in a card or note of celebration? There are many choices when you consider the underlying meaning of the event and other key issues.

## RELIGIOUS TRANSITIONS

The following occasions are religious rites of passage. They generally involve a party of some sort, and gifts are usually given. But even the most generous gift will be appreciated more when it is accompanied by thoughtful words from you.

### FIRST COMMUNION AND CONFIRMATION

Both Confirmation and Communion are Christian rites of passage, leading to full membership and participation in the Church.

Whether there is a Communion ritual and at what age depends on the denomination. Whereas Catholic children usually receive First Communion at age seven, for Protestant children, First Communion and Confirmation frequently take place together at a later age.

When writing to celebrate a Catholic First Communion, remember that you're supporting a rite of passage that indicates a child has moved into fuller participation in the life of the Church. He or she is now considered old enough to take part in a very important sacrament. Since you're talking to a seven-year-old, a short message is fine. An aunt wrote to her niece:

Dear ———,

*This holy day will give you memories you'll carry throughout your life and maybe share with your own children. May God's wisdom and love follow you.*

Or you might say something like:

Dear ———,

*Congratulations on your First Communion. This is a big step for my very special cousin. We're so proud of you on this wonderful day.*

Confirmation is the sacrament in which boys and girls formally come of age in the Church, confirming the vows godparents made for them at Baptism and choosing to take on adult responsibility for faith. It usually takes place between the ages of eleven and seventeen, depending on the denomination.

When writing a note for Confirmation, you can recognize the child's commitment and talk about confirming faith, making a decision, and taking on responsibilities.

One young woman told me, "I'm Lutheran and I received lots of Confirmation cards that included personal words like, 'Congratulations on this day on your accomplishments.' It *is* an accomplishment. You've made the effort yourself and consciously decided to accept Jesus Christ."

You can also write about what *you* value and try to say something personal about the youngster, as family friends did in this note:

*Dear* ———,

*You're making a commitment to grow and develop in the Church. We feel sure that in your life ahead you'll put Christ's precepts into action. We hope you find them useful, especially in your relationship to others and your community.*

*We've always included you as a member of our family, so we take pleasure in celebrating this special occasion.*

Another option: "I know this is a great day. You're an adult member of the congregation now. You're deepening your relationship with Christ and with the Church. My congratulations and love are with you."

## BAR MITZVAHS AND BAT MITZVAHS

A bar mitzvah is a rite of passage in which a Jewish boy becomes a young adult with new responsibilities in the community. Though the bar mitzvah dates back to the Middle Ages and has its roots in antiquity, the bat mitzvah, or coming of age for girls, is a twentieth-century ritual and takes place at many, though not all, synagogues. (Orthodox Jewish congregations do not hold bat mitzvahs.) Usually occurring at age thirteen, both bar and bat mitzvahs are joyous religious and social occasions that involve substantial planning.

When you write a note, "Congratulations"—or "Mazel tov," which literally means "May your stars be good"—are in order. Then you can add any other words that the heart may prompt. Feel free to write a secular message—or something religious (such as "May God bless you") if you are more inclined to do that.

You can talk about accomplishment because preparation for a bar or bat mitzvah *is* an achievement. The child attends religious school, learns a new language (Hebrew), and becomes familiar with the prayer book and how to lead the service. He or she usually writes and gives a speech at the service as well. In light of this discipline and learning, you can write, "I know how hard you've worked" to any youngster, because it's true.

If you're a close friend or relative, you can express pride in the child and mention the pleasure he or she has given you. One young girl told me, "I like hearing personal things like 'This bat mitzvah will be special for me, too, because I've known you since you were born.' It also makes me feel good when someone writes, 'I can't wait for your bat mitzvah.'"

When I wrote to one young woman, I recalled that she was a talented singer back in kindergarten, when she would perform for her parents' guests. I said:

*Dear* —————,

*You had star quality even when you were five. I'll never forget you belting out a song to entertain us. Now you shine more brightly than ever as a lovely, talented young person.*

*We can't wait to share this day with you.*

Since bar and bat mitzvahs reinforce connections and maintain family history and traditions, you can talk about family in your note. Or you can mention that the child is now recognized as an adult in the religious community.

You may have very specific feelings to discuss. One man told me, "I think the material aspects—all the presents and the party atmosphere—need to be separated from the real significance."

He wrote to a nephew:

*Dear* —————,

*After the gifts are forgotten, consider what this day really means—and the opportunities presented to you. This is a time to think about goals for the years ahead. It's your world and it's important to treat it wisely.*

*The future is yours.*

When you don't know the child well, you can also tie in the message to the gift, as I did in a card I wrote to a neighbor's grandson. My gift was a sports watch with numerals that glow in the dark. I wrote:

*Dear* ———,

*Now if someone asks the time at three* A.M., *you can tell them. Congratulations on your special day. Your grandmother told us how hard you've worked to be prepared.*

*Best regards,*

## JEWISH CONFIRMATION

This ceremony takes place at age fifteen or sixteen and marks the completion of a young person's religious training. It is more of a choice for a child than a bar mitzvah (which is considered mandatory in most Jewish homes), and you can talk about that as in, "Congratulations on reaching this milestone. We're delighted that you've chosen to be confirmed. You're very special to us."

## LA QUINCEAÑERA

A Quinceañera is a "coming out" ritual for Latinas everywhere on their fifteenth birthday. The celebration of becoming a woman begins with a ceremony at church, where the girl receives a blessing. A party, which is often as elaborate as a ball or a wedding, follows with food, drink, music, and dancing.

Quinceañera cards are available at many greeting card stores. Add a handwritten personal message, talking about the bright future ahead and including birthday wishes. Or mention how memorable the occasion is, as a family friend did in this note accompanying a gift of a music box:

Dear ———,

*Congratulations on this very important time of your life. The future lies before you. As you grow as a woman, follow your dreams.*

*I hope this gift will always remind you of your Quinceañera.*

*Love,*

## GRADUATIONS

Any graduation is a landmark event, signifying accomplishment, discipline, responsibility—and the beginning of the next step in life. A personal note, with or without an accompanying gift, is an opportunity to celebrate the achievement and to offer support for goals ahead.

Considerations include what graduation is taking place (high school? college? law school?) and the level of achievement. It's easier to find words for a top student, president of the class, or captain of the football team than for an underachiever. Age counts, too. Today you could be writing to an adult who returned to school at thirty-five or fifty or older, and recognition of the commitment involved could be especially relevant.

A good note can:

1. PRAISE ACHIEVEMENTS.

Can you talk about an academic record or honors or extracurricular activities like the debating team? Be specific. An aunt addressing her eighteen-year-old niece wrote:

*Dear ———,*

*I'm busting my buttons! You made it and made it big. Honor roll, winner of the French Club award, member of the tennis team—you've certainly achieved your goals.*

*You can't imagine the pride we feel in you.*

Most graduates aren't stars, however, and some have barely squeezed through school. But you can always find *something* to compliment, even if it's working hard at a job after school. Try something like: "We're so proud and happy about your graduation from [name of high school]. You've come through four important years in school—and out. Your mom told us all about the rock band you organized."

For a mature adult student, simply completing college or graduate school is a badge of merit. One woman told me, "A friend of mine went to nursing school at forty. She had children at home and it was really hard for her to juggle her responsibilities and stick with it. When she graduated, I sent flowers and wrote, 'We're so proud of you. You really hung in there with courage and determination. We feel privileged to know such a special lady.'"

## 2. LOOK AT THE NEXT STEP.

Is the graduate going on to higher education, the Peace Corps, or a job in a corporation or state government? One aunt wrote to her niece en route to the Navy:

Dear ———,

*What an exciting path you've chosen. We're so proud of you and your achievement and hope the Navy appreciates how lucky it is to have you on board.*

*We love you and look forward to hearing all about your new life.*

To a business major in college headed for a career with a brokerage firm, an uncle wrote:

Dear ———,

*Congratulations on your graduation. When you were eight years old you said you wanted to work in the stock market. Now you're on your way! I hope you get where you want to be and I look forward to lots of interesting conversations about mutual funds.*

To a drama buff, one could say:

Dear ———,

*I remember seeing your performance in* You Can't Take It with You *last year. I hope you have as much fun acting in college. Best regards.*

What can you say to someone who isn't ready to choose a career yet? How about, "Here's to a great year as a ski instructor in Colorado."

## 3. REFLECT ON GROWTH.

Graduation is a time to communicate respect for the person a child has become and trust in his or her potential. When a neighbor graduated from high school, one man wrote:

*Dear ———,*

*You've grown into a bright, dynamic young man with a keen sense of humor and the ability to laugh at yourself and keep life in perspective. It's a pleasure to see you moving on to [name of university].*

*You're going to make an important contribution wherever you go.*

And don't forget your own children. All youngsters look for approval on every level from parents. They want to know, "Did I make the right choices? Are you proud of me?" When her son graduated from medical school, a mother told me, "I validated his choices and who he is. I wrote about how proud I am that he's evolved into such a thoughtful and compassionate person—and what a fine doctor he's going to be. I think there's something special about the way he went to medical school and I told him that—how impressed I was that he was able to balance a new marriage and a grueling schedule, and still keep up other family relationships. I also said, 'I think you've made a great choice of a nurturing, loving wife.'" This kind of mirroring can be very meaningful to a child—at any age.

## 4. TALK ABOUT WHAT YOU VALUE.

A high school teacher focuses on the world the child is entering. He wrote to a former student, now graduating:

*Dear ———,*

*I hope you've developed both the knowledge and moral attitudes that will enable you to fight for what you know is right. This is a world with a lot of challenges. You can make it better. Best wishes.*

To a college graduate struggling with career choices, a family friend wrote:

*Dear ———,*

*Find fulfilling work, whatever it is. Be happy with what you choose. Do good, be kind, be true to yourself.*

*I love you a lot. Congratulations.*

Whatever your approach, an affirming or inspirational message from you can help add to the recipient's sense of self-worth and confidence. Don't miss these opportunities to mark important passages.

# Part 3

## Writing Notes

### for Difficult Moments

# Nine

## Get-Well Wishes

Years ago, I learned that a colleague of mine was hospitalized. She had been very kind to me when I was just starting out as a writer, providing invaluable guidance on several occasions when I needed it, and I wanted to express my concern. It was clear, however, that she was a very private person and I felt there was a fine line between saying, "I care" and intruding. With that in mind, I wrote this note to her:

*Dear ——,*

*Just want you to know I'm thinking of you. You're a swell lady and nobody else can give me the good advice you do.*

*Hang in there. I need you.*

A few weeks later, she wrote back to me, "Your note really picked me up. It was good for my confidence, which was considerably shaken, even though the heart attack was judged to be a 'minor' one. I am definitely getting stronger and more able to cope each day and hope to see you soon."

We all want to know that we matter to others and haven't been forgotten, especially when we're ill or incapacitated and feeling vulnerable. A heartfelt note is powerful medicine.

No matter how serious or sensitive the situation, there is much to say—and many ways to say it. Whether you're writing a separate note or adding a personal message to a greeting card (with or without flowers or a book), here's how to express your concern.

## Who Is the Patient?

Oddly enough, the more intimate your relationship with the patient, the less likely you are to write (unless you live far away). You'll probably be there at the bedside, in person, for a parent or child or spouse. On the other hand, you may reach out and send a card or note to a business acquaintance or a neighbor as a courtesy or out of empathy.

What you say depends in part on how open the patient is, how close you are, and the shared history you can draw upon.

## What's the Prognosis?

The patient's medical condition and how much you know about it will also affect the message. Will the person wind up good as new? Or is the situation life-threatening? Words and tone that are just what the doctor ordered for a tonsillectomy may be inappropriate for a stroke.

The most difficult notes to write involve situations where the outcome is unclear—or all too clearly negative. "Get well" either does not apply or can seem inadequate when someone lies gravely ill, is coping with a chronic condition, or is in for a long, uncertain rehabilitation. You can now find some commercial greeting cards that are sensitive to such scenarios, but you'll still want to add a personal message of your own.

## What Do You Want to Say?

Are you chuckling over a jogger who stepped in a pothole and fractured a foot, or in shock over someone who is critically ill? Whatever the diagnosis (and your reaction to it), a personal note makes a human connection. It reassures a patient who is anxious, stressed, and in discomfort to hear, "You are not alone. You are important to others. You are remembered." Just a few choice words can have a significant impact when it counts.

These strategies can help you communicate a meaningful message—in the context of what has happened—in your own individual way:

### 1. Try a Light Touch, When Appropriate.

You can't fix a knee joint or gallbladder, but you can take the person's mind off of it for a few minutes and perhaps bring a smile with a note. Some conditions actually lend themselves to humor. After I had bunion surgery, a friend composed a silly poem that made me laugh.

When a businessman broke his leg falling down the stairs at a ski resort, an associate wrote to him:

*Get-Well Wishes*

*Dear* ———,

*Obviously it's unsafe for you be anywhere near a ski slope. Since it looks like your slaloming days are over for now, hope you can hobble down to Florida (crutches and all) for the convention. You know it will be dead without you.*

*Heal with haste.*

Following back surgery, another patient received a bouquet of flowers with the message, "While you're convalescing, you may as well smell the roses. We love you."

Someone sent this e-mail when a businessman tripped and fell on a cracked sidewalk: "Dear ———, Heard you wound up with ten stitches in your forehead. Only you could hitch a ride to the emergency room in a police car. Please take care in the future."

A personal note to an associate who had to return to the hospital for a second operation read, "I know you liked the nurses, but this is ridiculous. Hope you are on the mend soon. We need you."

2. LOOK FOR YOUR POINT OF CONNECTION WITH THE PERSON.

My note at the start of this chapter conveyed gratitude to a mentor who had made an impact on my life. What is *your* link to the patient? Do you work or carpool together? Did you grow up together? The answer will lead you to associations you can use in what you write.

A message that connects can also mention specific qualities you appreciate. In writing to an acquaintance who serves on a volunteer committee with you, you might say:

*Dear ———,*

*Just want you to know that your good ideas and energy will be missed while you're in the hospital.*

*Best regards,*

### 3. MENTION A WELL ROLE MODEL.

Everyone who's sick wants a role model of well people. If you're writing to a coronary bypass patient, you can point to a public figure the patient admires or others you know who have recovered from the same surgery and are living full, active lives. You might even add something like, "I don't know how the doctors found anything wrong because I know personally that you have a very good heart."

When her eighty-year-old aunt had cataract surgery, a niece used the patient herself as a role model:

*Dear ———,*

*You sailed through your first cataract surgery and I know you'll do well with this eye, too. Remember, you're my favorite aunt.*

*Love,*

### 4. BE REAL.

A friend of mine suffered terrible injuries in an automobile crash years ago. In the hospital for months, she endured multiple operations, including several reconstructive procedures. I wrote over and over again to her, "I think of you all the time" or, "You are in my heart." And this, I believe, is the essence of what people want to hear, especially at times of calamity.

When my friend recovered, she told me, "I was showered with notes, and the warmth in all of them helped me get through this. My husband would read each one to me and I'd say, 'Put it up on the wall.' It was good to know people were praying for me, too, regardless of the religion. One note said, 'I lit a candle for you today at St. Patrick's Cathedral.' It helped."

People often don't know what to say in a desperate situation, yet a few words, when they're genuine and real, can make a difference. Remember that it isn't necessary to make the patient feel better. What matters is the message, "I care about you and I'm here." Acknowledge what has happened, without dwelling on it, and treat the patient as the same person you have always known. (In contrast, pretending the illness really doesn't exist creates distance and actually isolates the patient.)

An option for a friend on exhausting kidney dialysis might be, "Take one day at a time. Enjoy what you can. I'll see you next week."

## WRITING TO A CANCER PATIENT

Notes to cancer patients deserve special mention because the disease seems to affect so many people—and because we tend to think of cancer as deadly. Sometimes it is, but on the other hand, there are so many cancer survivors today.

What *can* you write? Again, that depends on how close you are and how open the person is. I would hesitate, for example, to write at *all* unless the patient (rather than a third party) has told me about the diagnosis. Many people prefer to keep their health histories private (often for professional, as well as personal, reasons).

"It bothered me a lot that a former neighbor I haven't seen in years wrote, 'I heard you're in the hospital with cancer and I hope you're doing well.' I didn't want the whole world to know about my cancer," a patient told me. She admits, however, that she would have felt touched by a note that read something like, "I heard you were in the hospital. I don't know the details, but I just want you to know I wish you well."

If the patient *has* confided in you, these techniques can help you write with sensitivity:

### 1. FILL THE PERSON WITH OPTIMISM.

If you know the prognosis is optimistic, you can treat a note as a message to get well: "Hope all goes well at the hospital. I look forward to seeing you as soon as you're up to visitors."

To a breast cancer patient you can say something like, "When I heard your news I was devastated. But then I think of all the women I see going on with their lives and doing so well. I hope you'll be joining that club."

### 2. AVOID "SHOULDS."

Acknowledge that the situation is difficult and, if appropriate, that the outcome seems to be bright—but omit words that imply that the patient has to do something about it. Statements like "You have to beat this" mean well, but they actually put pressure and responsibility on patients. If they don't get well, they feel they've let you down. Said a lung cancer patient, "Don't call me a 'fighter.' Then if I don't win, I'm a loser."

The trouble is, "shoulds" impose *our* views of what the patient ought to think and feel. They shut off communication by sending the message, "I don't want to hear anything negative."

To convey optimism without "shoulds," stick to "I." Talk about "I think" or "I feel." You *can* say, "*I feel* you're going to beat this." You can also try something like, "If it were me, I'd be a nervous wreck."

### 3. Address the treatment, rather than the outcome.

Consider something like, "I hope this chemotherapy period will go quickly." You can add, "I'm not sure if you want visitors or not. Would you like me to come over? I'll bring the Danish. Or do you feel up to going out?" (When someone is sick, the last thing they want to do is entertain *you*.)

Since some patients undergoing chemotherapy lose their hair and wear wigs, you can also say (if it's true): "I like the way you look in your new wig."

### 4. Give a goal.

You can write, "Our Labor Day picnic [or our daughter's wedding] will be complete if you can be there." This gives a goal without imposing responsibility on the person. Instead of, "You must be at my birthday party," try, "Somehow I know you'll be at my birthday party."

### 5. Just care.

To a relative who had a mastectomy, I wrote:

*Just a Note to Say . . .*

*Dear ———,*

*It hurts my heart to think of what a rough time you must be going through. I wish you healing ahead. You're on my mind always.*

*Love,*

When her cousin had a cancer recurrence, someone wrote:

*Dear ———,*

*This isn't fair. You've been through so much already. You're in my prayers.*

## OTHER PAINFUL SITUATIONS

When the outlook is bleak, try to connect with where the person is. For example, you don't want to say, "I hope you'll be back home quickly" if it is unlikely that the person will be leaving the hospital. But you can write, "I know this is a difficult time. My prayers are with you."

A message that is always meaningful is, "You've touched my life." I tried to say that when I learned that my neighbor was dying of AIDS. The ideal person to have next door, he was quiet, responsible, and always glad to lend an egg or a cup of milk when I unexpectedly ran out. Though we had a cordial relationship, we were not close friends. Yet I wanted to show my concern. I bought a simple card, blank inside, and wrote, "You're our favorite neighbor—actually the best we could ask for. Please know that we care."

What can you say to a coworker? Draw on your point of connection, as in, "I miss your particular brand of office humor." The person will know he or she has had an impact on your life.

To someone close who may be dying, you can relate a story about something special you've shared: "Today the hyacinths came up and I remember the day we planted the bulbs together." Or you might send a poem with a note saying, "I'm not good with words, but this touched me. I wanted to share it with you."

Offer help if you really mean it. But don't promise more than you're willing to deliver. You're going to *want* to do more for a dear friend or relative than for someone you know casually. You might write, "I'll call Friday to see if I can drop off a pie that you or your visitors might enjoy."

## MISCARRIAGE

Miscarriage is the spontaneous end of a pregnancy of less than twenty weeks. It is usually experienced as a devastating loss, surrounded with sadness, disappointment, and grief—although others sometimes minimize what has happened. Feelings of emptiness and isolation are common; the person may feel guilty that something she did caused the miscarriage.

I would not write at this time unless I was a close friend or the person actually told me what happened. In that case, however, words of support and acknowledgment of the pain and loss can be very helpful, as in, "My heart breaks for you. Remember, I'm here with a strong shoulder and anything else you need."

Because miscarriage happens to the couple, not just to the wife, it's appropriate to include the husband in your message. A man wrote this note to a couple he's known since childhood who suffered through a second miscarriage:

> Dear ———— and ————,
>
> I know you're both devastated and I'm devastated for you. This is something only time and love can heal. I wish there was something I could do.

In expressing his own helpless feelings, he conveyed great empathy. In fact, the couple told him they felt relieved to hear his words. They were then able to open up and talk about their own pain.

"I don't know what to say except I love you [or I care about you]" is also right for this situation. In one line it affirms the depth of loss.

## CHRONIC ILLNESS

Someone suffering from the effects of heart failure, arthritis, or another chronic illness will always appreciate a note or card on a good day or one of the bad ones. Try something like:

*Dear* —————,

*I'm so sorry you've hit a bad patch. You've had more than your share of ups and downs. Just want you to know I'm thinking of you.*

Or e-mail:

*Dear* —————,

*I hear you're coming along, and I wanted to say hello. You've been a rock through so many difficulties. You deserve good news for a change. You're on my mind.*

E-mail is perfect for regular "check ins" with people chronically ill or going through long recuperations to say, "I'm sorry you're hurting" or simply, "I care." One-liners that show support include: "How are you managing?" or "How is today going?" When a friend of mine was laid up with sciatica for three weeks, I sent e-mail messages every few days, such as, "How is your aching back?" and "This too shall pass. The upside is, now you can watch soap operas."

E-mail works, too, on the eve of a treatment, as in, "Best of luck tomorrow," or "I hope the surgery on Tuesday makes a difference for you." People feel nervous before any procedure or treatment and appreciate good wishes. E-mail also doesn't require the person to engage in conversation as a call does. Some of us want to talk on the phone at a difficult time, others do not.

To show support in a big way, consider organizing a blitz of e-mail good wishes from friends and coworkers. A barrage of get-well messages is like a bouquet. It's bound to give the person a lift. However, all these e-mail suggestions work only if the patient can access a computer and checks e-mail regularly.

## REMEMBERING FAMILIES AND FRIENDS
## OF THE PATIENT

Close relatives of someone who is ill experience enormous stress and deserve attention. Yet they are often forgotten. One mother told me that she received only two notes and few phone calls when her daughter was diagnosed with cancer. She couldn't believe it and felt so disappointed that she told her husband, "Maybe we need new friends. I've been writing to other people all these years. How could they be so thoughtless?" Her daughter was treated and is now doing fine. But the point is, you give a gift when you acknowledge a parent's or grandparent's anguish and pain. Just a few lines make a difference:

*Dear ——,*

*I can't imagine how difficult this time must be for Amy, and for you and Tom. I pray that all goes well.*

*All of your friends are thinking of you.*

I e-mailed someone who had three friends diagnosed with cancer in the span of a few months: "You have too much on your plate. I can't imagine how hard it must be to get this latest bad news. Please try to take care of yourself."

The possibility of losing these people so important to her was a blow to her own sense of connection, well-being, and security. I wanted to express words of support and understanding.

This note comforted a woman whose dear friend lay in intensive care:

*Dear ———,*

*You've told me often that Mary is like a sister to you—the sister you never had—and that you can't imagine life without her. Just want you to know I'm here any time you need a shoulder.*

*Love,*

I e-mailed these words to a colleague I did not know well: "——— told me about your husband's heart attack. I'm thinking of you both." I wouldn't have sent a handwritten note, but an e-mail seemed right.

## WRITING TO SICK CHILDREN

Ill and hospitalized children love getting mail, and the idea is to write cheerful messages that accent the positive. For young children who can't read yet, you can send kisses on a card. Just apply lipstick thickly to your lips, then imprint. To a niece recovering from pneumonia, an aunt wrote a little poem: "Hugs and kisses and a big red balloon. / I'm really hoping you'll get well soon."

If the illness isn't chronic or catastrophic, kids also need to hear hopeful messages of "This won't last forever. This pain is only temporary." You can say, too, "It must be hard to be in the hospital."

Consider mentioning what helped you get through an illness or injury. When her daughter had surgery for scoliosis, a mom made a list of the ways she coped when she had the same surgery as a girl. Her note included positive suggestions, such as, "(1) I talked on the phone to friends; (2) I cried."

"It's okay to cry" is a validating message for children, but do avoid statements like "You're a brave boy." Youngsters often think "brave" means they shouldn't cry.

Some of the best mail comes from teachers who ask everyone in the class to sign a card addressed to the patient. (The ill child invariably has great fun checking out who signed on.) Another idea: send photos of a family gathering, along with a simple message, such as "We really miss you" or "We're looking forward to you coming home." These words make children feel they're important.

Whatever you write, be selective when choosing get-well cards for children. Many feature sad faces—on bears or lions or balloons. The idea is to express sadness that the child is sick, but these images only reinforce negativity. To convey a positive message to the child, choose a laughing clown or happy dog instead.

Phone calls can invade privacy, arriving at times when the patient is resting or in pain. Because they require an immediate response and interaction, they place a responsibility on the patient. But no one is ever stressed or annoyed by receiving a thoughtful note, which can be read at leisure—and reread over and over again. A note is a special and permanent reminder that people care.

*Get-Well Wishes*

# Ten

## Condolences

I've always felt inadequate at funerals and condolence calls, never knowing what to say to the bereaved. Since words seem like awkward clichés, I usually stick to "I'm sorry" or skip language altogether, simply pressing a hand in acknowledgment or, if I know the mourner well, hugging the person. The same discomfort used to extend to writing notes of condolence. What do you say to a friend who has lost a beloved mother? To someone whose husband had a fatal coronary at thirty-five or whose twin sister died?

I often felt at a loss for words until several years ago, when I had to write a condolence note for a tragic situation. An acquaintance had suddenly lost a seventeen-year-old son. The boy wasn't sick; there had been no warning. He simply didn't wake up one morning. It was any parent's worst nightmare. What could be more painful than losing a child—a child for whom you had so many hopes and dreams, who was supposed to outlive you? It was unimaginable.

And that's exactly what I wrote. In my note to this mother, I said, "I cannot imagine what you are going through. I just want you to know my thoughts and my heart are with you." I simply signed my name.

That was one of the most difficult notes I'd ever had to write. Yet even in less tragic circumstances, condolence notes pose a challenge to virtually all of us. In our youth-oriented culture, death is a taboo subject we usually tiptoe around. Even the vocabulary makes us feel uncomfortable, which is why we rarely mention in a note that someone "died." Instead, we rely on more palatable terms like "passed on" or "passed away."

A death also stirs emotions in *us* that we'd rather not confront. There are fears about our own mortality and losing our own loved ones that make us feel vulnerable. No wonder we become anxious and blocked when searching for the right words.

A friend once confessed to me, "Sometimes I become so paralyzed, I keep putting off a condolence note and wind up not sending one—even though I know how important it was for me to hear from others when I lost someone close."

Yet there are ways to overcome discomfort and demystify the task of expressing sympathy. The secret lies in exploring issues nobody ever talks about and following some useful guidelines. Try them, and you'll never feel tongue-tied by a condolence note again.

## WHY ARE YOU WRITING AND TO WHOM?

One reason condolence notes intimidate us so is that mere words seem inadequate and futile. Since nothing we do or say will change what has happened, we feel helpless. But we rarely take a look at why we are writing. The goal is not to change the reality or banish someone's grief. The purpose of a condolence note is to express your sympathy, acknowledge the loss sustained, and, sometimes, offer comfort.

How you go about it depends largely on your relationship with the bereaved and with the person who has died. In the example earlier, the parent I wrote to was a casual acquaintance. We spoke cordially once or twice a year, over a period of many years, at business-related functions. I was not in a position to offer comfort because I didn't know the mother intimately—and had never met her son. But I *could* express sincere empathy and support.

## WHAT ARE THE CIRCUMSTANCES?

Any death produces a variety of emotions in survivors, including sadness, remorse, guilt, and sometimes anger. But the most devastating deaths, say experts, are those of a child or spouse. A tragedy like the one I described is hardest to bear not only because it involves a youngster, but because it is so sudden. There is no chance to say good-bye. Deaths from suicide or AIDS often add an extra dimension—that of stigma—to an already painful situation.

Such circumstances also provoke reactions in us. I would not have written my note if a more expected death—such as that of the recipient's elderly mother—had occurred. But the death of a child is different, and I felt I could not ignore such heartbreak.

The words flowed because for the first time, I looked deeply into myself instead of looking away. I felt my own sense of horror at what had occurred. I thought about my own children and how inconceivable it would be to know they were gone forever. Then I drew upon these human feelings that connect us all.

The death of a police officer, fireman, or someone serving in the armed forces in the line of duty speaks to us all, as well. And we can write exactly what we feel in a few simple words: "———— was a hero [or heroine] who gave his [or her] life."

## What Do You Want to Say?

A meaningful note is a way to say good-bye to the person who died and/or communicate with those who survive. When you really care about the people involved and what has happened, you can express deeply felt emotions like love, admiration, sorrow. When writing out of obligation, the point is still to touch someone.

The approaches below can help you find words that matter and make sense in view of the situation. If you don't know the bereaved well, keep the message short. Save lengthier, more intimate notes for people you're close to.

1. If you knew the deceased, talk about him or her.

Many of us hesitate to talk about the person who died, believing we will only intensify the pain of the bereaved. But in fact, the opposite is usually true. Mourners' greatest fear is that people will forget the loved one ever existed and that his or her memory will die with the person.

"When my son was killed, I *wanted* to hear about him. I *wanted* notes that confirmed what a fine person he was. These brought him to life for me," says the mother of a twenty-four-year-old auto accident victim.

She especially appreciated notes from his friends that spoke words like these: "Jim was one of a kind. When we went camping in California last summer, he was the environmentalist. He gave me a crash course in animal and plant life and raised my consciousness. He was like that, always prodding you to think and learn. His loss leaves a hole in my life."

A meaningful note memorializes the person who has died and indicates to the mourner, "Yes, I knew your son." It signifies what the loved one's life was all about, often through memories and anecdotes. The bereaved can then hold on to that note, look at it, and feel, "My child [or husband or parent] made an impact."

When an old and dear business-related friend died in his eighties, I wrote to his widow and children after the funeral:

*Dear ———, ———, ———,*

*Some people are larger than life—and Ben was one of them. We have such wonderful memories of him filled with fun and laughs, in and out of the annual conventions.*

*Ben's funeral was one of the richest I've ever been to because there was so much to say about this special man. We'll miss him always.*

*We send our deepest condolences.*

The better you know the deceased, the more you have to write about. When a woman lost a dear aunt, she wrote to her cousin:

*Dear ———,*

*Aunt Sue took care of me as a little girl, always with kindness and attention. I was treated as her own. This morning I remembered she was the one who taught me to put on nail polish—and how excited and grown up I felt. Memories like these keep her alive. Your sorrow is my sorrow. I loved her, too.*

When her best friend died of heart disease, a schoolteacher told me, "Judy and I had worked together and laughed together. Our families were close and we spent many weekends together with our children. In my note to her husband, I tried to talk about what we both had lost. I spoke about the person she was, about her strength and her ability to find humor in the most absurd and painful situations. She never complained and she was very forgiving. She dealt with life by finding the light and the joy, even when times were darkest. That positive attitude was a key to who she was. I wanted her husband to know what an important part of my life she was and that she will always be in my heart."

A pediatrician told me about a very close relationship he had with the mother of his best friend. She had all but adopted him, encouraged him throughout his growing-up years, and was the major influence in his decision to go to medical school. She continued to act as a mother to him even after he reached adulthood. At her death, he wrote this note to his friend (her son): "Don't mourn her death. Celebrate her life because she influenced so much of what we are today and lives on in our memories. I loved her and always will."

In a case where I had met the deceased just a few times, I was still able to find something significant to say based on what I had been told about him. I wrote to a close friend who had lost his stepfather, a man he cherished:

*Dear* ———,

*I know that [name of deceased] grew to mean a lot to you over the years and was more than just a stepfather. He aged in a way we wish for all of us, with dignity and enjoying life to the fullest.*

*Having met [name of deceased], I feel sad at his loss, too. I send my deep condolences.*

2. BE AS SPECIFIC AS POSSIBLE.

You can capture in your note the essence of the person who has died by describing his or her unique characteristics. Use words such as gentle, talented, kind, outspoken, caring, diligent, sparkling, fun, intelligent, dynamic, sensitive, loyal, courageous.

A lawyer wrote to the widow of a colleague who died after a long illness:

*Dear* ———,

*I was sad to hear that Joe passed away. In many ways, he was an original. He was often opinionated, particularly about food and wine, but always a delight to be with. He was a consummate artist in the practice of law and we all learned from him.*

*He will be missed professionally and personally by all who knew him. My thoughts are with you.*

Another woman wrote to her cousin:

*Dear —————,*

*When I think of your father, I always think of laughter. Uncle Bob was probably the funniest man I ever met and I loved listening to his latest jokes and observations. His humor will live in his children. I'll remember him in my prayers.*

You can also focus on the deceased's passions:

*Dear —————,*

*You spoke of your mother so often. Your face would light up when you talked about her lovable eccentricities—and her winning streaks at bingo. I remember you telling me what a character she was and how special.*

*Please know that I am here for you.*

### 3. RESPECT THE PROFUNDITY OF THE PAIN.

Each person believes his or her grief is singular—that no one else can know this particular loss. Without realizing it, I validated the pain of a grieving mother when I wrote in my note, "I cannot imagine what you are going through." I was right; I could not know. In contrast, it's important to avoid statements like "I know how you feel," which can make some mourners very angry.

People may also resent being told how they should or will feel, as in, "Eventually the pain will fade" or "You never really get over it." When her daughter died of meningitis, a mother complained, "People keep telling me, 'You must feel angry.' I don't want anyone telling me what I must feel. I want respect that my grief is private." Then what *can* you say? If you don't know the person well, "I can't imagine your pain and sorrow. I grieve for your loss" is eloquent and enough.

If you're close, you can say, "You gave all that you could to [name of deceased] for ——— years. I hope you will remember what a loving, caring parent you were." Parents especially may feel guilty that they couldn't protect the child and may need validation.

It's also wise to avoid sharing accounts of your own grief when you lost a loved one. Something like "I remember the pain I felt when my own mother died" may seem like a comforting thing to say, but it actually shifts the focus away from the mourner at a time when he or she is entitled to your total attention and sympathy.

Similarly, when a newborn dies, people may comment to the parents, "You can have other children." A loss is a loss, however, and either early or late in life, people aren't replaceable. Be sensitive to the person and genuine. To someone close, you might try something like, "I know how much this baby meant to you. My thoughts are with you." Otherwise, you can never go wrong writing simply, "I'm thinking of you at this time of sorrow."

When a twenty-eight-year-old lost two grandparents within a few months of each other, he received this note from friends:

*Dear ———,*

*We were shocked to hear of your grandfather's death. What a horrible year for you. It's hard enough to lose one grandparent, let alone two in the space of six months.*

*We're thinking of you in sorrow and sympathy.*

Whatever the situation, skip platitudes, such as "The good die young" or "He's in a better place." The mourner may not feel that way. It's also wise to avoid mention of an afterlife or "God's will" unless you know the person well and are sure he or she is religious.

4. VALIDATE THE EFFORTS OF THE BEREAVED, WHEN
   APPROPRIATE.

After her sister died of cancer, one woman wrote to her brother-in-law, who had been "a bulldog at the bedside." She began her note: "You did everything possible for Tess. I saw the love and support you gave. No one could have done more to protect her."

You can also capture something special about the mourner's relationship with the deceased. Says an arts consultant, "When people have told me they appreciated my note, it's because I was able to do this. I have a friend who went to law school late in life. When her mother died, I wrote, 'I know your mother derived great pleasure from your accomplishment. She talked so proudly of you.'"

Limit such comments on the relationship of two other people, however, to situations where you know them very well and are absolutely certain of the facts. For example, this mother *could* have thought a return to school late in life was a waste of time. A widow or widower *could* have been less than devoted during a spouse's illness. An adult child may *not* have provided appropriate support to an elderly parent.

### 5. If offering help, be specific.

It's become routine to write, "Please let me know if there's anything I can do," but don't offer unless you mean it. There's nothing worse than an insincere gesture, and if you really want to help, mention a specific task. (Otherwise you may never be contacted.) The bereaved have their world turned upside down and can't think of delegating or organizing. Yet day-to-day life must go on and there are little things people don't have the energy to do. Say, "Let me shop for you" or "Let me walk the dog [or take the children to school]. I'll call tomorrow."

---

### OTHER LOSSES

"When my closest friend died last year, I felt devastated," an executive told me. "Somehow friends aren't considered a loss the way relatives are. But it's a big deal and needs to be acknowledged. Friends are important, especially if you're single."

The fact is, if someone you work with dies, there's a natural support system. People are together in the workplace every day and can be there for each other. There may be a special memorial service. But the death of a friend is often overlooked, even though caring words can make a difference. The executive above was enormously touched when her sister sent a card and wrote inside,

---

"I'm so sorry about the loss of [name of friend]. I'm sure having you as a friend was a great comfort to her."

The death of a pet can also be traumatic, though this can be hard to understand if you aren't a pet lover yourself. There's a tendency to feel that an animal isn't a person. But, like a special friend, your dog or cat loves you whether you get a promotion or not, whether you have a killer tennis serve or not, and even if you've gained ten pounds. This kind of unconditional relationship is hard to find, and owners feel deeply about their pets and mourn them.

Says a dog owner, "Corky was my first dog and I loved her to pieces. When she died, my friend sent me a lovely little note mentioning the nice memories she had of her. She wrote, 'I know it must be hard for you, but remember, Corky had a good life.' I was so moved that she appreciated that it *was* a loss in my life. Sure, it's not like losing a child or a parent or a husband, but I felt very sad. Receiving that support was very nice."

## SPECIAL CASES

When suicide occurs, it's common for family members to feel rage at the self-destruction as well as a sense of loss, shame, and guilt. There are thoughts of "If only I had recognized the signs" or "If only I'd intervened." This is another time when a message like "I can't imagine how you're hurting" is always appropriate. You can also comment on caring behavior you know about, as in, "I know you were at the emergency room several times."

On the anniversary of the death of a friend's brother from AIDS, one woman wrote, "Not a day goes by that I don't think of the way you took care of [name of brother] during the last months. I'll remember your love and courage always."

These honest words fit when a death could have been avoided, as in the case of a medical mistake: "This shouldn't have happened. There aren't any words to console you, but it may help to know I am thinking of you."

Whatever the circumstances, write condolence notes promptly. Sometimes life intervenes, but do your best. Putting it off won't make it any easier to deal with, and the bereaved need to hear from people quickly.

In cases where you must write a very belated note (for example, six months after the death), consider writing something that is positive and looks forward, as in, "I drove by your house today and thought of you. I hope things are going well." If you wish, you can add, "Let's get together for coffee. I'll call you."

A social worker once told me, "In our society, death is the only stage of life where words fail us." But that doesn't have to be so. A meaningful note closes a relationship with someone who is gone and opens the door to the living. The key is found in the heart.

## E-MAIL AND CONDOLENCES

As a general rule, do not e-mail condolence notes. The medium does not convey the significance or connection of a handwritten note or a personalized card. It can seem to trivialize what has happened. However, e-mail is acceptable when you wouldn't otherwise express sympathy. For example, a consultant sent this e-mail to a client's assistant:

*Dear* ———*,*

*I'm sorry to hear of your mother's death. I am thinking of you at this sad time and extend my condolences.*

The consultant explained that he wouldn't have gone to the trouble of sending a condolence card. The relationship didn't merit it. But the assistant had helped him on occasion, and he felt moved to acknowledge the loss when he could do it so conveniently. Because the recipient didn't expect to hear from this person, she appreciated the gesture.

An e-mail response is also appropriate when someone has told you about a loved one's death via e-mail. Of course you want to reply, "I'm so sorry." If the person is important to you, however, follow up with a condolence card or note in the mail.

E-mail is useful, too, to stay regularly connected with someone who is grieving. It takes a long time to heal, and just the words, "Wondering how your day is going," can make a difference.

You'll find additional information and many more examples of condolences in my book *My Deepest Sympathies: Meaningful Sentiments for Condolence Notes and Conversations, Plus a Guide to Eulogies.*

# *Eleven*

## *Support at Times of Disappointment and Trouble*

Life can be difficult, but your caring words can reassure someone that he or she is not alone and that bad times won't last forever. The trigger may be something relatively minor, as when you e-mail, "How awful was the root canal? I know it's the worst. Feel better." Or you may wish to make contact at a time of serious emotional pain.

### GETTING FIRED OR LAID OFF

Losing your job can be devastating. A note in the mail or a sensitive e-mail provides comfort. Someone wrote to his brother: "This is a bad break, but it's their loss. I love you, bro." Or try, "There's life after Smith & Jones. Hang in there. This is only temporary."

When someone's hoped-for job or business deal falls through, say something like:

*Dear ———,*

*I know this is a disappointment, but I have every confidence you're going to land on your feet. How about lunch on Tuesday?*

*Love,*

## DIVORCE OR BREAKUP

When relationships break up or don't go well, people appreciate support from those close to them. The failure of a marriage is not an "occasion" and there are no rituals surrounding it, yet even parties who *want* a divorce feel a profound sense of loss—and grief. Everyone concerned needs comfort and connection. You don't write, "Gee, it's terrible to hear about your messy divorce." But good friends are a safety net. You can convey hope and reassurance that the person will get through this.

Someone who has been divorced herself has written many of these notes and can speak with the power of direct experience. One of her notes read:

*Dear ———,*

*I'm sorry to hear about you and Bob separating, but I hope things will turn out best for both of you. Sometimes change has a way of making us move in directions or make choices that we wouldn't have thought of. I hope you'll find what's right for you. Change can be very positive, though you may not feel that way now.*

*May you heal soon.*

This four-word e-mail from a dear friend meant a lot to someone whose divorce just became final: "To a new start. Love, _____"

One woman felt devastated when her fiancé left her just a week after the engagement party. She appreciated this e-mail from a close friend, which told her she was loved after all:

*I know you feel shell-shocked, but he didn't deserve you. Much better times lie ahead. I love you.*

Here are some other messages that can be used for a divorce or the breakup of a serious romance:

*"This has not been fun, I know, but the sun will shine again."*

*"You've been through a lot. I'm proud of you."*

*"Love was blind. That was then, this is now. Let's go shopping and celebrate a new day."*

*"I know this is a painful time, but I'm here for you."*

*"To launch the next part of your life, let's have dinner. My treat!"*

If you're not a very close friend, but still want to express support, play it safe with something like, "Just want you to know I'm thinking of you. Hope [year] is a happier one for you."

## SUPPORT FOR A CARETAKER

The caretaking role is a stressful one, often laced with crises. Encouraging words give welcome support. I sent this e-mail to a friend who felt devastated that she had to put her father in an assisted living facility:

*Dear ———,*

*I know how you've agonized over this decision, but you've done all you could. You've been a loving daughter and arranged for the best possible care. Please call anytime you need to vent.*

When life is painful, it means a lot to know that others care about you. Is there someone who would appreciate your words of support right now?

# Part 4

## Writing Notes for Other Occasions

# Twelve

## Thank-You Notes

*Florence dear—The best party of the summer. Thank you. Everything was perfection, especially that terrific chocolate dessert. More!*

*I absolutely love the nightgown and robe set. The colors are sensational! I can't wait to see you at my bat mitzvah.*

*Dear ——————,*

*My birthday was unforgettable. I suddenly felt a warmth in my heart that turned into bliss. Thanks for sharing my joy, being part of the celebrations of my life—and for the beautiful address book and planner. You can be sure I'll give it a workout.*

We've all heard the mantra from our mothers: "If someone can take the time to send you a present, you can sit down for a few minutes to write a thank-you note." But what many of us *didn't* learn from the lectures is how to write notes that sound genuine and real. Too often we settle for one-size-fits-all messages like, "Thank you for your lovely gift. It was very thoughtful of you."

How can you rise above platitudes and generalities that give the impression you're getting a chore out of the way? The answer is not to dazzle with witty words; it's to be authentic and say something meaningful in the context of the situation—as I felt the notes above did. Written to me by a neighbor (in the first case), the daughter of a business associate (in the second), and a friend (in the third) they made me glow and feel appreciated.

Here's how you can say "Thank you" and show that you sincerely mean it.

## STRATEGIES THAT WORK ANYTIME

Though thank-you notes are not always required (depending on the situation), they are always welcome. Those that are special say you were touched in some way and make a connection. They tell people you enjoyed their hospitality, liked a gift, valued a favor. They also say, "I appreciate *you*."

Of course, you sometimes don't feel especially grateful or care deeply about the people you're addressing. Everyone has obligations at times and some notes involve simple politeness or courtesy. Yet they also bind us together, and you may as well make them as significant as possible.

One man expressed his sincere sentiments in just nine words after receiving a bottle of wine as a thank-you for helping out a colleague: "So much for so little. Thank you very much."

What else can you say? Regardless of the circumstances, there's more to write about than you realize. These guidelines can help you get in touch with positive thoughts and feelings and express them:

1. FOCUS ON WHAT THE PERSON GAVE.

Was it assistance (like providing the name of a good dermatologist or helping you move into an apartment), an experience (like an insider's tour of a city), emotional (or other) support that made a difference, a tangible gift?

One note read:

*Dear ———,*

*Thank you so much for the beautiful pen. It is greatly appreciated, although unnecessary. It was my pleasure helping you.*

*I'll think of you every time I write a check!*

*With much love,*

Another note said:

*Dear ———,*

*My beautiful silver starfish cufflinks are just what I need for my new blouses. Just wore them for the first time and already got a compliment. Thanks for having such good taste and being so thoughtful.*

At the very least, you can describe the item or situation—and, when possible, sound enthusiastic. One man did so in these words: "The cigars were a great gift, but the braces are even better. I will show them off as coming from a friend who would, and did, give me the 'shirt' off his back."

Write in a lively fashion not about "the birthday gift" but about "the luxurious ivory sweater that feels so soft (no itching!) and looks great with so many things in my closet." Mention how you're going to use it, as in, "I'm planning to wear it this weekend."

## 2. ASK YOURSELF WHAT MADE IT IMPORTANT TO YOU.

How do you feel about the item or kindness? One note read: "Thank you, thank you for the stunning flowering plant. It's unusual and gorgeous, and really adds life to my (still) only partially furnished apartment. You must tell me where you got it. It certainly brightened my birthday. I will always remember your thoughtfulness."

Following a visit from an old friend, a lawyer in the hospital for knee surgery wrote:

*Dear ——,*

*I can't tell you how much I enjoyed seeing you. I needed a lift and your visit yesterday was a shot in the leg! That was present enough, but you also brought that thoughtful book. I can't resist spy thrillers and look forward to reading it.*

*Best always,*

After I took someone out to dinner for her birthday, she wrote: "What a friend! I had a great time with you at my birthday dinner.

I treasure our time together—there's so little of it. Thank you for making my birthday very special."

These words thanked someone for lunch: "What a wonderful afternoon I had sharing 'wise woman' stuff! It was just what I needed to put my daughter's move to Florida in perspective. I felt truly 'celebrated' for my birthday. Thanks for a memorable lunch."

3. REFLECT BACK TO THE PERSON.

You can also talk about how the gift or event reflects a specific personal quality of the giver, such as creativity or a sense of style, as in, "The lilies were pink and white and beautiful. With your eye for color, only you could have sent them."

Did your mother-in-law buy many lavish Christmas gifts for your preschooler? You might write something like this to her:

*Dear ———,*

*You've put Santa Claus to shame. [Name of child] adored everything you sent, which was enough to keep six children happy. You've always been a generous, loving grandmother (and the best mother-in-law I could ask for), but you've outdone yourself this time.*

*All my love,*

Another note focused on the host's horticultural talents: "We've been to two of the nicest gardens in the world—yours and Giverny. Thanks for a wonderful time."

## 4. TELL THEM WHAT THEY WANT TO HEAR.

Like everyone else, I want to know I pleased my guests and that a gift I bought was on target. Implicit in the notes I received were the messages, "You succeeded. You're a good hostess. You made a good choice."

I try to keep these points in mind when composing my own notes, which is why I often write something like, "It's always a treat to spend the evening at your house" or "Nobody throws parties like you do" to a host or hostess.

And who wouldn't want to hear, "What a gorgeous crystal bowl. As usual, your taste is exquisite."

## 5. LIGHTEN UP.

There's always room for a smile in a thank-you note. After a friend gave me the use of her resort condominium for a week, I wrote:

*Dear ———,*

*We had a swell time. The apartment was ultra comfortable and convenient, the weather cooperated, and we enjoyed every minute of sun and fun. You give new meaning to the word "hospitality."*

*Now if you'd only buy a town house in Paris . . .*

These words would make any recipient smile:

*Dear ———,*

*The first glass was superb. The second was sublime. Thank you so much for the best brandy I've ever had.*

## 6. Do your duty.

Do you plan to return (or exchange or give away) the platter you don't like or need? Keep the information to yourself when you write. That doesn't mean you should tell a lie (though some people do). You can always find something positive to say. Often, it's what you leave out that makes the difference.

For example, you can describe the gift, but skip mention of how you will use it. Switch the focus, instead, to the giver, as in, "The brass buffalo is truly special and unique. You obviously took much time and trouble to find such an original piece for our anniversary. Thank you for thinking of us."

## Tips for Common Situations

### Weddings

Writing thank-yous after such a big event can be a full-time job, and individualizing them for large numbers of people can drain the most energetic newlyweds. (Fortunately, many grooms share the note-writing responsibilities these days. He writes to his family and friends; she writes to hers.)

No matter who holds the pen, however, the goal is to let the giver know, "I remember *your* present—and it matters to me. I also remember *you*."

This kind of note makes the giver feel his or her gift was appreciated:

*Dear ———,*

*Thank you so much for the excellent fish poacher. Fred and I look forward to trying our hand at cooking something more* elaborate than broiled salmon and stretching our culinary skills. We can't wait to use it.

It meant a lot to have you share our day—and meet Fred in person. Much love and thanks.

These words combine enthusiasm for the gift and sincerity.

Dear ———,

The crystal frame is absolutely beautiful! We immediately raced to our photo album to pick out a photo to display in it. As always, you chose a gift that really means something to us.

Thank you.

Another note says, "You helped get us started on entertaining":

Dear ———,

Thank you so much for the flatware place settings. Once we fill in the china, we'll be ready to entertain in style. Thanks also for all your support and good wishes during these past few months.

All our love,

A second-time bride wrote:

Dear ———,

I've always been a good cook, but my dishes have never looked like this. The French casserole is simply beautiful and seems to make everything taste better, too! I use it all the time.

*I'm so glad I had the opportunity to finally meet you at the wedding. [Name of groom]'s mother has talked about you often. We look forward to seeing you again soon.*

At another wedding, small cameras were placed at each table. All the guests had a wonderful time taking photographs and the couple wound up with hundreds of pictures, some of which they enclosed with their thank-you notes. One note to a relative read:

*Dear ———,*

*Thank you so much for the gorgeous silver tray. It's such an elegant way to serve and I've already used it with pride.*

*[Name of groom] and I were so glad to see you at the wedding. It was an unforgettable day for us and I'm enclosing a photo of your table, so you can remember it, too. (You do look marvelous in that red dress!)*

When the gift is money, say how you're going to spend it. (I personally do not feel comfortable mentioning the amount, though it is considered proper etiquette to do so.) A groom wrote:

*Dear ———,*

*Thank you so much for your generous check. It made a big difference in our life. We really needed a car (public transportation leaves much to be desired in our area) and Helen and I used it toward our new blue [name of auto]. It is cool!*

*Most of all, thank you for joining us on our big day. We've been busy moving to our new home and hope you will come spend an evening with us as soon as we're settled.*

⚶ Thank-You Notes ⚶

Notes for shower and engagement gifts would be generally the same, perhaps concluding with a phrase like, "Can't wait to share our special day with you."

Try something like:

*Dear ———,*

*Thank you so much for the magnificent Waterford vase. It was the first engagement gift Michael and I received, and we were so excited to open it. It will always have a special importance and prominence in our home.*

*The wedding planning started out in high gear. We're so happy that you two will be sharing this occasion with us.*

To thank a group of workers who gave you a bridal shower, how about: "What a team! Thanks to all of you who helped make my shower such a surprise. You sure know how to keep a secret. I'll always remember what you did."

## Hospitality

Whether you're a guest at a formal dinner party or you spend the weekend at a friend's beach house, you can always glean something specific from the occasion. When you remember the event, see what highlight jumps out in your mind. You can talk about the great time you had (if true) and/or comment on the care taken— the hard work and attentiveness to detail, the menu and presentation, the atmosphere. Discuss the selection of guests, how nice it was to meet interesting new people, the stimulating conversation. If you felt pampered or were sorry to see the evening end so quickly, say so. Nothing pleases a host or hostess more than hearing that the guests didn't want to leave.

What can you write after spending a few days in the country with the parents of your new "significant other"? Try something like:

*Dear ———— and ————,*

*A thousand thanks for welcoming me into your warm home last weekend. I loved spending quality time with you and your family. I now understand where Steve gets his quick wit and sharp sense of humor.*

*The food was delicious, the company dynamic, and I enjoyed meeting all of your friends. Thanks again for your gracious hospitality.*

*Fondly,*

After Thanksgiving dinner at a friend's house, a young couple wrote: "We always feel lucky to be included in your family celebrations. We had a wonderful time. Thanks for inviting us once again."

When my husband and I were entertained like royalty on a business trip to Texas, one couple was especially kind, taking us on a tour of "ranch country" and inviting us to their house. I wrote this note to them:

*Dear ———— and ————,*

*Texas hospitality is legendary and now we know it's no myth. What a wonderful week. We've never felt more welcome and especially enjoyed the delicious Friday-night buffet at your lovely home. (How did you know Mexican food is our favorite?)*

*It was a pleasure to meet your family and friends. Please give us a chance to reciprocate and show you around New York soon.*

After spending time in Maine with friends, an executive assembled an album of photos she'd taken during her stay and sent it along with this note:

*Dear ———,*

*Thanks for making my first visit to Maine so memorable. You opened your home to me and made me feel totally comfortable. The meals were incredible (I can no longer fit into my clothes) and it's been a long time since I've laughed so much.*

*The consequence is I can't wait to come back. You'll notice I've left room for more photos of my next visit. Love from a grateful guest.*

Sometimes, however, you need all the imagination and powers of diplomacy you can muster. There's the case of one woman who had just moved into a community and was invited to brunch and a card party by a neighbor.

"I was the fourth at bridge and I didn't play as well as the others. They all wound up yelling at me, including the hostess. It was awful," she says. Yet she felt she still had to acknowledge the event. She wrote, "It was thoughtful of you to invite me to the bridge party and give me the opportunity to meet your friends. I'm really sorry my game wasn't in your class. Thank you for including me."

If the dinner last night was a disaster, you might like this solution. Finding the food unpalatable and the other guests obnoxious, one man focused his note on the attractive table setting and added, "The people were riveting."

## BABY GIFTS

When the present is clothing (and the baby has already worn it), mention how he or she looked, as in, "What an adorable outfit. It arrived yesterday and [name of baby] wore it today. He looked *so* cute." This note is descriptive and full of spirited warmth:

*Dear* —————,

*You are so thoughtful. I love the incredible jacket from France you sent for Iris. It's so chic and I can't wait until she is big enough to wear it. Your taste is perfect.*

*I was touched by your note. It's hard for me, too, to believe I'm a mother. We are enjoying every minute of parenthood and hope you'll get a chance to meet Iris very soon.*

*Much love and thanks.*

If the gift is a toy, talk about how it is being enjoyed (or will be) by the child, as in, "The crib toy you sent is already keeping [name of baby] busy. She can't take her eyes off it." Or, "The stuffed elephant is cute as can be. There's no doubt [name of baby] will love cuddling it."

A new mom and amateur photographer wrote:

*Thank-You Notes*

*Dear ———,*

*Thanks so much for the adorable photo album you sent for Billy. It's so cute and we will fill it with photos in no time. We have been taking lots of pictures. To see some of them, check out the Web site we designed—[address of Web site].*

*We appreciate your kindness.*

Depending on how much you want to write, you can also convey news about how the infant is progressing, as in: "Max is growing like crazy. So many changes in just over a month. His eyes are open all the time and he's two pounds heavier and an inch longer. Of course we think he's an amazing baby." Mention how siblings (if any) have reacted to the new arrival. One new mother enclosed a picture with her note, adding, "I'm sending this photo so you can see [name of baby] for yourself. She is as sweet in disposition as she is beautiful."

## GRADUATION GIFTS

Only people who truly know and care about you are likely to give you a graduation present. They deserve sincere words of appreciation.

A high school graduate thanked a family friend this way:

*Dear ———,*

*Being a poor excuse for a fashion statement, I have very few presentable articles of clothing. Formal wear is a pair of jeans without holes in the knees. The sweater you sent is just what*

*I need for my trip this summer and for those occasions at college when I can't look like a bum. You can only go so far in a T-shirt and sneakers.*

*Thank you so much.*

A new college graduate wrote this note:

*Dear ——— and ———,*

*As always, you are there for me at the special times in my life. I appreciate your graduation check, which will be a contribution to my "moving out" fund. See you at Thanksgiving.*

*Love,*

## CHRISTMAS GIFTS

Tell people that the Christmas gift they gave you was one of your favorite presents this year, and you can be sure they will glow. Try something like: "You're a mind reader! How did you know [name] is my favorite author? Can't wait to read [title]."

Or how about this note to a client, customer, or colleague:

*Dear ———,*

*Your delectable basket of goodies arrived and we've already sampled most of it. You picked our favorite cheeses.*

*Thank you so much for thinking of us every year. Have a wonderful holiday.*

I wrote to a friend:

*Dear* ——,

*Your absolutely delicious fruitcake arrived and it's already half gone. Who could resist!*

*Thanks so much for remembering us. Have a great holiday and let's have dinner in the new year.*

## SPECIAL EFFORTS

If someone works for you as a volunteer, praise the person and the effort. Then he or she will come back and work for you again. After I organized a program for a professional conference, the chairperson wrote to me:

*Florence:*

*It was a smash—and I wasn't surprised. Whatever you touch turns out right!*

*So many thanks for one of the best programs ever. You woke me up at 9 A.M.*

*Regards,*

Will I say yes the next time she calls for my help? Of course. Words like these will also please people: "Thank you for being so generous with your time, experience, and expertise. I really appreciate it and hope I can help you one day." Or, "Thank you for all your help and encouragement at the conference. You really made us look good."

## WRITE PROMPTLY

Whatever the occasion, send a thank-you note as soon as you receive a gift or very shortly thereafter. That may be difficult with thank-yous for wedding gifts, due to the volume of notes you must write, but even the sincerest words sound hollow when you write them long after the gift has arrived. Certainly send your notes within three months. People expect this courtesy and also want to be certain their gift was actually received. All it takes is a few lines.

## E-MAIL AND THANK-YOUS

An e-mail thank-you is not acceptable for gifts, most cases of hospitality, or important favors. If you have any doubt about using e-mail, don't. Sentiment is trivialized by the technology, and remember, it's a note or card in the mailbox that gets attention and says that you have manners and care.

It's become accepted practice to e-mail a thank-you note after a job interview. However, your e-mail is one of many on the person's computer. If you want to stand out, mail your thank-you letter.

However, e-mail is fine to thank someone for watering the plants yesterday (or walking the dog), or another casual favor, as in "Dear ———, You were right. The guy who designed your Web site is very reasonable. Thanks for the recommendation." Or, "Your advice about talking to my father was very wise. I had lunch with him as you suggested, and am so glad I did. Thanks."

I have on occasion e-mailed appreciative words to members of a committee I chaired, such as, "I can always count on you for innovative ideas, thoughtfulness, and hard work. Thanks so much for your great work on the committee."

By all means e-mail a thank you in cases of online relationships. After meeting a man online, then in person for the first time, a friend of mine always e-mails a message such as, "Dinner was great last night. Thank you. Let's do it again." If she isn't interested in seeing the person again, but he did buy drinks or dinner, she still e-mails something like: "I enjoyed meeting you for margaritas. Thank you. Good luck in your online search." Her philosophy is, "He was a gentleman. Why not extend this courtesy?"

## ACKNOWLEDGMENTS OF CONDOLENCE NOTES

I appreciated this handwritten note from a friend's mother, whose husband had died:

*Dear* ———— *,*

*My heartfelt thanks to you for your gift to the scholarship fund at [name of college]. Since this fund bears [name of husband]'s name, you have honored his memory.*

*Thank you for all your caring. Your note with fond memories of [name of husband] also meant a great deal to me. Many thanks and warm regards.*

A note can also mention appreciation for warm words, comfort, prayers, companionship, and/or support at a time of grief:

*Dear ——— and ———,*

*Your touching note arrived after a particularly emotional day of closing up my mother's apartment. It's a very odd feeling saying that good-bye. I guess one is never quite prepared for the finality of it all. Thank you for remembering Mom with your contribution to The American Cancer Society. Having good friends like you is truly wonderful.*

In a belated note, a grieving son wrote: "Although this is way past due, I want you to thank you for your lovely note. It's such a comfort to know that our friends understand what we've gone through and are there to offer support."

Regardless of the situation, people appreciate acknowledgment of their gifts and efforts. They want to hear they've pleased you. With just a little extra thought, your written thanks assure them that it's true.

# Thirteen

## Holidays

Christmas without Christmas cards? Valentine's Day or Mother's Day without a message in the mailbox? It's unthinkable for many of us, since connecting with others is integral to celebrating holidays like these. Yet because we often feel expected to write (if we don't respond, we feel guilty), the effort to send cards and notes can become a chore. Writing can in fact be pleasurable (even fun)—if you find a way to make each message unique, personal, and different from year to year. To do that, consider variables such as what the holiday means to each of you and what's going on in your lives.

## CHRISTMAS

Years ago, my best friend in college married an officer on a nuclear submarine. From then on, she lived on U.S. Navy bases in faraway places, and we went years without seeing each other. But every Christmas, her annual greeting arrived in the form of a newsletter full of family details, bringing me up to date. It was obviously sent to a long list of people, but she always added a few handwritten lines for me, chatting about possible get-togethers in the future, mutual friends, and concluding with something like, "I miss you. Hope this year brings all your heart's desires."

For my friend, as for many others, Christmas greetings—lengthy or brief—are an opportunity to touch people, share news, and play catch-up. They're a chance to reconnect with those who live elsewhere or whom you haven't seen as much as you would like. What can you add to a printed card or message that makes it truly personal? Mention something specific that will have meaning to the recipients.

One option is to write something like, "I could not let this season go by without connecting with you." Then refer to a memory that brings a smile or a moment you've shared, as in, "This morning I was remembering the weekend we spent at the beach last summer. Too much time has gone by since then. Let's get together soon."

A friend wrote, "May the joy of the season put a blush on your cheeks. It's that time of year again." Then, to connect with someone who had given her new ideas for tree decoration, she added, "You should see my Christmas tree. Your tips were great!"

Someone else sends her own homemade candies every year to friends, along with a card saying, "Have the sweetest Christmas" or "Merry munching!"

You can also personalize with something like, "Hope you're enjoying your new apartment [or baby, or car, or computer]. Merry and happy everything at your house."

In a card to a couple taking tango lessons, someone wrote, "May you glide through this season in health and happiness. P.S. How are your dancing feet?"

One couple enclosed a photo of their three-year-old son in their card and also referred to a previous conversation with the recipients about preschools. They wrote, "From our house to your house—Merry Christmas. How lucky we are to have friends like you in our lives."

Others reflect on what being a family is all about. One young woman admitted, "This year, I've been a brat at times." In a card to her mother, she wrote, "Thanks for being there even though I know I've put you through some high drama. All your understanding and support mean a lot to me. I love you. Merry Christmas."

While Christmas is regarded as a secular, social occasion by some, it remains an intensely religious event for others—a time to express deep beliefs with spiritual meaning. In this case, messages usually discuss prayers for peace or the birth of Christ, or reflect on the ongoing responsibility to bring Christ into the world.

Whatever Christmas means to you and yours, remember that the choice of cards is part of the personalization process. An executive sends jovial cards to the festive people she knows and "season's greetings" cards to those who don't observe Christmas. For others who are devout, she visits a museum shop for cards featuring reproductions of fine religious art.

Personal messages on Christmas cards are a great way to thank colleagues and coworkers for their support. A manager wrote:

Dear ———,

*Just a voice from the wilderness telling you what a great job you do all year long. My friends are jealous of me for the support I get. Merry Christmas.*

Another message read:

Dear ———,

*Can't believe that it's almost ten years since we started working together. Of course you were (and are) a person with unequaled vision! Merry Christmas to you and your family.*

To thank a secretary or assistant, try: "I can't tell you how much your help means to me. Merry Christmas." Or, "Thank you for your loyalty and support throughout the year. Happy Holidays."

I sometimes respond to Christmas newsletters or cards that include family photos with a note such as:

Dear ——— and ———:

*You guys sure know how to take great pictures. Who snapped them? Wishing you all a splendid Christmas.*

Or,

Dear ——— and ———:

*We always enjoy receiving your cards and watching your beautiful family grow. Be proud!*

Or,

*Dear ——— and ———:*

*Wishing you and those beautiful boys a wonderful holiday season. I get updated information on how you're all doing from [name of grandparents]. You're obviously fabulous parents.*

## Tips for Christmas Newsletters

A pastor's wife who writes her own newsletter every year says, "Christmas is a time to focus not on all that's wrong in the world, but on all that we have to be grateful for—our families and the solace of friendship." I've based this advice for Christmas newsletters on what she told me: Write your newsletter to share meaningful family news and connect. Mention that Jill is playing soccer, Bobby takes trumpet lessons, a new baby is on the way in April. Talk about how the kids are growing and learning and adjusting at their new school. Or announce that you're thinking about retirement. Discuss your volunteer work or even your book club's latest choice.

Avoid bragging about achievements and possessions—that your son got all As on his report card, your daughter is valedictorian or head cheerleader or prom queen or you're buying a bigger boat. The message "Look how smart and wonderful we are" does not capture the spirit of the season or bring people together. In fact, it may separate you. Other families may have children who are struggling in school or have other difficulties and aren't winning popularity contests. People want to know that Billy's leg is finally out of the cast, not that Sissy is reading already at age two. If you won a hot dog eating competition, however, that's different.

## HANUKKAH

The eight-day celebration of the Festival of Lights, Hanukkah is a joyous Jewish holiday that commemorates the Maccabees' victory over the Syrians in 165 B.C.

You can simply say something like, "I hope this is a special Hanukkah" on a Hanukkah card and add a personal reference to friendship or family connection, such as, "It's been ages! I'm counting the days till we visit in January."

Or you can reflect on the fact that Hanukkah is a time of warmth, special foods and traditions (such as lighting Hanukkah candles), and festive gatherings. You might write something like, "May the Hanukkah candles light up your life." Then add something specific to the person, such as, "P.S. Thank you for showing and sharing your wisdom last week. Looking forward to dinner on Tuesday."

A note I received from old friends read:

*Dear Florence,*

*Hope you are having a happy and well-fed Hanukkah holiday on [name of our street]. We are! The girls are home from college and we're getting to spend some time together. Miss you!*

*Love to all,*

Another note mentioned a traditional Hanukkah food:

*Dear ———,*

*From our home to yours we wish you a Happy Hanukkah filled with love, joy, peace, and potato latkes. You're in our thoughts.*

*Love,*

One woman receives handmade "books" for Hanukkah from her grandchildren every year. With titles like "Thirty Great Things About My Grandma," the books feature loving details about Grandma's potato pancakes and how nice her kitchen smells when she bakes cookies. Even if you aren't a kid anymore, perhaps there's a message of appreciation you'd like to write to someone close to you.

## KWANZAA

This seven-day African American holiday focuses on the importance of family and community. Each day, beginning on December 26, one of the following principles is celebrated: unity, self-determination, collective work and responsibility, cooperative economics, purpose, creativity, faith. Candles are lit, gifts exchanged, and dinners or parties are held as well. Special foods, such as corn, nuts, fruits, and vegetables, are also served during this observance, which is linked to African harvest festivals.

To mark the occasion, one man wrote to old friends:

*Dear ——— and ———:*

*This is such a meaningful time for me to honor our heritage and traditions—and I know how special it is for you, too. Enjoy the celebration with [names of children].*

*Can't wait to see you all this week.*

A message can also talk about themes like peace and the joy of community.

## NEW YEAR'S

A new beginning, a fresh start, high hopes, promises to make positive changes—all of these are associated with the new year. Do these images (and thoughts of the person you're addressing) stir feelings in you? You may want to express them in a message.

Each year, someone sends a New Year's card featuring a meaningful quotation, such as:

*The real voyage of discovery consists not in seeking new landscapes but in having new eyes.*
*—Marcel Proust*

Then a few personal lines follow:

*Dear ——— and ———:*

*I'm working on a fresh outlook for [year]. I haven't forgotten you and will call soon to set up a date to catch up. Regards to the family. Have a happy New Year.*

I sent this note to a close friend who had suffered professional and health setbacks:

*Dear* ———,

*What a year! Let's hope you don't see another like it again. But it does clear the way to what matters—such as telling you how fortunate I am to have you as a friend all these years. Here's to a happier, healthier [year].*

A New Year's card to an editor about to have knee surgery read:

*Dear* ———,

*May [year] be a safe, simple, and prosperous year filled with great books. Hope you're back on your feet fast.*

I wrote to a colleague who had retooled and become a food writer: "Now that you've reinvented yourself, you deserve a spectacular New Year. Here's to lots of great assignments (and cookbooks?) ahead."

Someone else wrote:

*Hi* ———,

*This year I resolve to spend a lot more time with you than last—and show up on time, too. I think of you a lot. Hope the New Year is a kind one—and productive.*

Another option: choose a New Year's card illustrated with champagne glasses or a bottle of the bubbly and add, "To a vintage year for the whole family!" Or simply write "Hope this is the best year ever for you."

## JEWISH NEW YEAR

Rosh Hashanah is the Jewish New Year. It ushers in ten days of introspection, culminating in the most solemn day on the Jewish calendar, Yom Kippur, the Day of Atonement. You can add to a card, "Have a happy and healthy New Year" or "Shana tova" (which is Hebrew for "a good year") and add something personal, as in, "Thinking of you and our many years of friendship. All good things for the New Year."

One note I received read, "It's always a comfort to know you are our dear friends. We wish you a sweet New Year." (Honey and sweetness are associated with the New Year.) And this message from a non-Jewish friend made me smile: "Have a meaningful Rosh Hashanah."

This holiday is a time for reflection on the year past, the future, and on themes such as mortality. If you feel philosophical, it's also appropriate to talk about hopes for peace and understanding.

## RAMADAN AND EID

Islam's two major holy festivals are Ramadan and Eid. Muslims throughout the world pray, feast, and fast (between sunrise and sunset) during the monthlong holiday of Ramadan. A handwritten "We know this is a time of reflection and devotion. We wish you and yours a blessed Ramadan" is appropriate for a note or a personal line on a greeting card.

Eid is the day of celebration following the last day of Ramadan. People exchange gifts and visit friends and families on this occasion. A personal message might say, "Happy Eid to you and yours. We are thinking of you at this time of rejoicing." Or, "Enjoy warm and wonderful times with your family. Best wishes for a joyous Eid."

You can find cards in English and Arabic in ethnic or UNICEF stores and in some general greeting card shops.

## VALENTINE'S DAY

For me, Valentine's Day is pure fun and a good excuse to express affection to anyone I care about. If the spirit moves you too, let yourself go and compose something playful.

One year, I thought "red," after reading that red is the biggest seller in roses for Valentine's Day. I wrote to my husband: "Red means love, red means passion, / I will always love you, in my fashion. XXX." I like writing silly poems when the mood strikes me— and my husband loves receiving messages that make him smile.

Any spouse, whether working in the business world or not, will enjoy hearing, "The bottom line is: I love you always."

Or maybe you feel more serious. One woman cried at these words from her significant other: "I can't tell you what the last eight years have meant to me. You've been the best part of my life and you've made me very happy. All my love on Valentine's Day and every day."

Another note read: "Nothing is guaranteed in this world, except my love for you. Happy Valentine's Day."

A husband added this message to a Valentine's Day card to his wife: "Sweetheart, we both married well. I love you."

You don't have to limit your Valentine messages to a spouse or romantic interest. Chances are a friend, family member, or even a close colleague would love to receive an unexpected message of caring. (Children and teachers actually receive most of the Valentine cards.) A grandmother I know enclosed a small amount of money in a card and wrote to her grandson, "Buy yourself a treat because you're so special. Love you a lot." One woman even sent a Valentine's Day card to her sister, who was enjoying a booming social life. She wrote: "Love is in the air. This is your year to *really* celebrate Valentine's Day."

A true romantic wrote, "My heart beat faster when I met you. Still does." The next year he used this quote from the Song of Solomon: "How much better is thy love than wine." Then he added, "You're my one and only."

A travel agent sent his girlfriend a gardenia plant, especially welcome in the month of February. The gift card read, "This is almost as beautiful as you are to me. Love, ———"

And how about this note that a young woman wrote to her boyfriend on a card with a golf motif: "You drive me crazy. I love you on Valentine's Day and all year long." Try it for any golfer you're wild about.

# EASTER

Easter is one of the three most popular holidays for sending cards. (Valentine's Day and Christmas are the other two, according to Hallmark.)

The central event of the Christian faith, Easter celebrates the Resurrection of Jesus and also the hope of new life. These themes can be incorporated in a personal message. Since Easter is a time for family gatherings and going to church together, references to the pleasure of family may also feel right.

But some of us are more reflective than others. If for you, Easter means spring, bunnies, and decorated eggs (Easter eggs symbolize renewal), you might feel comfortable with something like, "Happy Easter. New life is all around us." Just add a comment specific to the person, such as, "Can't wait to see the new pink hat you told me about."

## MOTHER'S DAY

*Dear Mom,*

*You are the best and certainly deserve more than one day of recognition. Any woman who can give me nine months of free womb and board deserves a medal.*

*Love, love, love!*

*Dear Mom,*

*We hope you like the flowers. You deserve a lot more than a dozen roses. But this is all we can afford.*

*Dear Mom:*

*We know that sometimes you wish you had daughters, but we do the best we can. Much love. Happy Mother's Day.*

These notes from my sons are etched in my heart. Mother's Day is special to me, and the truth is, I'd feel devastated if my children didn't remember me in some way. It has to do with my identity, and I am not alone. Mother's Day stirs unusually strong feelings in virtually all the mothers I know.

Yes, I know some people consider Mother's Day a commercial stunt. But if you love your mom and know it will mean a lot to her to hear from you on Mother's Day, you may decide to make her happy in spite of your own views. What can you write? Acknowledge what she means to you and/or show appreciation for what she's done, as a daughter did in this note:

*Dear Mom,*

*As the years go by, I have learned to love you more and more. Thank you for all your love and support through the good times as well as the trying ones.*

*P.S. [Name of husband] loves you, too.*

A stepdaughter wrote:

*Dear ———,*

*I want you to know you are quite a woman. I hope that someday I will be as intelligent and compassionate as you are. The love you've given to Dad and me in the last two years is cherished.*

*Happy Mother's Day.*

And let's remember mothers-in-law. A daughter-in-law wrote:

*Dear ———,*

*You have become very dear to me over the years, and since my own mother's death a tremendous source of support and solace—even when I don't see you for a while.*

*Thanks for too much to count and for being a truly wonderful mother-in-law and grandmother.*

*Love,*

Or simply try, "Hallelujah, it's Mother's Day! Have a great one, Mom."

## FATHER'S DAY

One man told me, "My wife cries if the kids forget her on Mother's Day. But I don't care about Father's Day." My husband shares this lack of interest in the holiday. Yet many other dads I've talked to feel differently. Says a divorced father, "I'd be crushed if my children didn't remember me on Father's Day. Maybe it's because I don't see them every day and I'm very concerned about having a good relationship with them, but it's important."

Father's Day is an opportunity to acknowledge your dad's place in the family and a time to say, "Thank you for being my parent." Your words can be powerful even (or perhaps especially) if your relationship has ups and downs. A son wrote:

*Dear Dad,*

*On this Father's Day, I want you to know how much I respect and love you. I know that I don't express that feeling very often, but perhaps it's because I am so much like you. Both of us keep the good thoughts bottled up inside.*

*Tomorrow might see us fighting over some inconsequential matter again, but for today, let it be known that my father is a special man.*

*All my love,*

Someone else wrote to her father, as he made a comeback from a serious illness:

*Dear Dad,*

*This is a special Father's Day because it's so good to see you up and around and enjoying life again. Here's to healthy times ahead.*

*I love you.*

*Holidays*

Minor holidays also present an excuse to write, as in "Happy Halloween and have a haunting good time. Did you buy your pumpkin yet?" Trading pumpkin pie recipes or pumpkin decorating tips is a pleasurable, fun thing to do. We're all so busy and harried these days that it can be hard to find time for the people we care about. This is one way to do it.

Holidays can be stressful. Yet these occasions also reinforce connections between family members and friends. Sincere words give expression to something significant in their lives and yours.

# Fourteen

## Good News

*Just heard Tommy was accepted at medical school. You always wanted a doctor in the family.*

*Read about your transfer in* The Wall Street Journal. *I'm glad things worked out the way you wanted.*

*Congrats on the new country house. That takes care of your weekends!*

Life is too often a struggle, which is why it's nice to notice when sunshine peeks through for people important to us. Whether major or minor, good news is a chance to share a positive event or salute those we care about (or members of their family)—and lift our own spirits at the same time. One-liners like "Nice job!" or "Well done!" or "Great news!", followed by a mention of what has happened, can work for many situations. Here are other ways to say, "I recognize how important this is" or "I know how happy this makes you."

# PROMOTIONS

When someone has advanced in rank or responsibility, he or she appreciates kudos and words of encouragement. In cases where the person has reached a top position, how about "Hail to the Chief! You're going to be a great director of research."

I wrote to an editor I've worked with for years:

*Dear ———,*

*Congratulations on your promotion to editorial director. It's about time. To a brilliant future.*

*Best,*

When a friend was promoted to executive vice president, I wrote:

*Dear ———,*

*No wonder this came through. You're good for anybody's business. Congratulations.*

Someone promoted to director of sales appreciated these words from his sister: "Obviously you're a star! I'm so proud of you."

## AWARDS AND ACHIEVEMENTS

To recognize a special award, mention it by name, as in: "Congratulations on winning the Man of the Year award. You should have been honored years ago. You are a role model for everyone in this business." You can also discuss the person's talents and qualities (such as intelligence, vision, and initiative) that contributed to the honor.

Mention experiences you've shared too. When his partner celebrated twenty-five years with the company, a man wrote:

*Dear ———,*

*No one has had a more profound impact on [name of firm] than you. You've set the course that has led to our growth and success. We've had our storms and temporary setbacks, but we've come through because of your leadership. It has been— and still is—exciting to be part of the [name of firm] experience.*

*Wishing you many more happy, productive years,*

*Affectionately,*

Sometimes it's the person's child who has achieved. I wrote this note to the mother of my son's classmate in nursery school. The boy, now all grown up and a talented painter, had his first show at a major art gallery. I wanted to say, "Yes, I understand. I'm a mother, too."

*Dear ———,*

*My heart skipped a beat when I saw the announcement card for Peter's show. You must feel so proud. I see that sweet lanky boy at nursery school and remember him well. It's such a joy to see how wonderfully he's turned out. You certainly did something right.*

*I plan to see the show tomorrow. I'm excited for Peter and for you.*

*Regards,*

I e-mailed friends whose daughter is an actress: "Saw Mary in [name of show] last night. She was wonderful, of course." What parents don't appreciate applause for their children?

And don't forget encouraging words for less dramatic, but still important, personal accomplishments. Did your best friend lose weight? E-mail, "Twenty pounds is an achievement! I'm awed that you're lifting weights twice a week at the gym." This works, too, if your brother stopped smoking, as in, "Eight weeks without a cigarette is an achievement!"

## NEW JOB

A mom wrote these words to her son when he started a challenging new job: "You always exceed my expectations. I'm bragging to all my friends about your new gig. Good luck."

"You always make me proud," would be another way to put it. Or how about this message for virtually any relationship: "Opportunity has knocked! Good for you."

Today, people retire and may later decide to return to a paying job. Someone offered support in this e-mail: "Much luck on the new position. I know you're nervous, but remember how good you really are." Another possibility: "Welcome back to the workforce. Wishing you the best in the new job."

Sometimes a positive happening doesn't quite fit the category of "event," yet acknowledging it is a nice thing to do. An author received this note: "I was delighted to see your new book in the enclosed catalog. Hope you're selling thousands! All good wishes." An e-mail to the same person read, "What a kick to see your great review in *Publishers Weekly*. Their sales forecast should make you very happy."

Someone else sent a pertinent newspaper article to a colleague and wrote: "This is a great plug for you and your company. Bravo!"

This e-mail acknowledged an ad for a new line of products: "Read the announcement for your beauty aids in the *Herald*. Just what every woman needs! Bet they sell like crazy."

Or how about this stroke in the form of an e-mail to a parent or grandparent: "Just saw on local TV that Karen's soccer team made it to the championships. I always said she was a winner!"

Another e-mail supports the recipient and also builds confidence: "Loved your talk at the meeting last night. You always say it like it is." Such words are especially nice to hear because most of us feel inadequate as public speakers and don't really know how we come across.

These words confirm a wise decision: "How smart you were to buy that condo. Did you see the rising prices in today's real estate section?"

*Good News*

## RETIREMENT

Retirement, which caps a lifetime of achievement, deserves a salute, as well. Write about the person's career achievements and accomplishments and express admiration—or talk about his or her plans for the future, such as spending more time on a beloved boat or taking adult education courses. Humor is always welcome, as in this note to a retiring government official:

*Dear ———,*

*We voted unanimously not to accept your resignation. Try retiring again next year.*

*With admiration,*

This e-mail tickled someone else: "I'm so glad you're retiring. Now we can all go to the movies in the afternoon."

## NEW HOME OR APARTMENT

Whether you're writing a note to accompany a housewarming gift, or simply congratulating someone on moving to a larger apartment, stimulate ideas by thinking about what the change means to the person or couple. Surrounding a move are feelings of excitement, anticipation, and possibility. You can talk about hopes for the future, as in "Congratulations on your new apartment. May it be just the beginning of great times ahead."

Or tie in to a housewarming gift, as in, "Now that you finally have a backyard, can a barbecue be far behind? Hope you enjoy these steak knives when you grill." Or try, "These wineglasses should help you celebrate your new home." If you're really stuck, talk about the extra space in a larger house: "Now you can move your office out of the closet." Or you can always fall back on geography, as in, "Hope you're settling in to your new cottage in Connecticut. Best wishes from all of us." When a casual communication seems appropriate, e-mail something like, "Congratulations on your new pad." Or simply say, "Best of luck on the big move."

Good wishes share the joys in life—large and small—and encourage those we care about. All it takes is a line or two to make an impact and touch someone's heart.

# Fifteen

## More Reasons to Write a Note

*All we get are bills and junk. People like to get personal mail. Just a handwritten envelope with your name on it. It's so warm, it's so nice.*

It's the American way to wait for a special occasion to write, but any day is a day to recognize friendship, express love, and acknowledge tender moments that might ordinarily slip away. In fact, many of the best notes emerge "out of the blue." Spontaneous and free of pressure, they're often fun to write because the person is not expecting to hear from you.

At other times, words can lend important support. We all want attention and it feels good to be remembered. Words can also bring us closer together.

Opportunities to connect through a note are all around you, hidden in thoughts that make you smile, flashes of insight, warm feelings that might be shared. The idea is to become more aware of these small moments and recognize their value. Here's how to seize opportunities to write a note that might pass unnoticed—and be more expressive when they arise.

## AFFIRM A BOND

"Every now and then, a close friend I've known for years sends me a note saying how important my friendship is to her. These notes move me because they just come," says an acquaintance of mine. One note read, "I was thinking about you today and the fact you're somebody who brings joy to my life. I treasure your capacity for optimism (which is infectious), your understanding, and your ability to slice through to the heart of the matter. The truth is, I've never met anyone like you. A friend like you is rare and precious."

One man, who keeps in touch with his older brother by mail, told me, "I sent Matt a baseball card recently because when we were kids, the Major League star on the card appeared at a local department store. We were first on line to get signed autographs and it was a big deal for us.

"I didn't have to say much on the accompanying note; the baseball card was a reminder that we share a past. I mulled over how I felt, thought of who we've both become, and wrote, 'Isn't it amazing to be adults and have kids and be parents. I miss you.'"

So many caring feelings are often left unsaid—especially to the people we love most. A note like this one refers to a shared consciousness and says, "Remember?"

Notes can also say, "You touched my life"—sometimes to people you've met only briefly. I think of a time when I found myself alone in another city and looked up a journalist I barely knew. We spent a wonderful afternoon trading information on the writing life. Later she wrote:

*Dear Florence,*

*I'm glad you took the initiative and let me know that you were in town. I so enjoyed our visit.*

*Since I saw you, two of the projects we talked about got the green light and I'm circulating other ideas. You inspired me!*

A simple e-mail can help cement a new bond. Following dinner out with a couple my husband and I recently met, I e-mailed,

*Dear ———,*

*We had a swell time last night and enjoyed meeting your husband. Let's arrange an encore soon.*

## BE PLAYFUL OR CHATTY

I could never forget a vacation with my husband in Puerto Rico years ago. After lounging at the pool all afternoon, I returned to our hotel room and discovered a gorgeous bouquet of tropical flowers waiting for me outside the door. Attached was a note: "Couldn't help noticing you at the pool. Are you free for dinner tonight?" It was left unsigned.

A secret admirer? Yes—my husband. It was his way of adding a little romance, and it made me laugh; it made me glow; it made me

feel desired. The note was more important than the flowers—
something tangible in hand that said, "I love you."

On the other hand, someone else wrote, "Thanksgiving turkey
and the bottom coil of my oven blew out. And yours? Here come
the holidays and I'm thinking of you."

E-mail is an ideal way to share an interesting or fun experience—right away—as in, "Dear ———, I just spent an hour at
our favorite activity, shopping. Bought a great dress on sale. What
a coup. Next time let's go together." Or, "You must read this new
book I just finished." Or, "Just saw the jewelry show at the
museum. Don't miss it. Wait till you see the brooches."

## STAY IN TOUCH WITH SOMEONE FAR AWAY

It's difficult to keep finding fresh things to say when writing regularly to a child away at college (or at summer camp), in the armed
forces, or working in another state. But it takes only a line or two
to make contact on a postcard, particularly a picture postcard, or
via e-mail. Send or e-mail photos of the family or clippings from
the local newspaper that will interest the recipient, such as articles
about the neighborhood school or the neighbor's dogs. Just add a
line or two saying something like, "Thought you'd get a kick out of
this. I miss you. Love, ———".

One woman stays in touch with grandchildren far away by occasionally sending little fun gifts (under two dollars) with just a
short, "Hugs and kisses from Grandma."

You can also collect and use anecdotes about people or events the recipient can relate to, as in, "I looked up your old pal Jimmy on the Internet. Can you believe he's married and has three kids?"

What you say matters less than the fact that you make contact. It's hard to think of anything more nourishing than the warmth of words from home.

## APOLOGY

A few years ago, I was invited to a friend's house for dinner. During conversation with other guests, I gestured a bit too enthusiastically with my arm and knocked a crystal goblet off the table, shattering it. I wrote her a note thanking her for a wonderful evening, then added, "I'm mortified that I broke your beautiful goblet. Please forgive me. I'm trying to find a replacement."

Who doesn't say or do something insensitive, insulting, or otherwise regrettable at times? We're all human. A quick, sincere apology can usually soothe hurt feelings or heal a rift and even strengthen your relationship. Apology is also tremendously freeing for the person who offers it.

It's best to apologize in person, on the phone, or in a note in the mail. But if those options are just too intimidating, try e-mail. E-mail is perfect for very minor apologies, such as: "I'm so sorry I had to cut our conversation short yesterday. It was one of those days. How about putting a date on our calendars for lunch?" But e-mail is also a way to repair relationships. It removes some of the awkwardness of apologizing, acts as a "buffer," and allows you to say exactly what you need to without interruption.

Simply write, "Forgive me for barking at you yesterday" or "I'm sorry I blew up at you. I was really out of line." Or, "I apologize for showing up 30 minutes late for our dinner date without calling. I'm sorry I was so inconsiderate." Or, "I apologize for introducing you incorrectly at the birthday party. I should have been more careful."

Incidentally, do not say, "I'm sorry you felt hurt [or put down or insulted]." That is not an apology. The implication is there's something wrong with the other person's perception, rather than with your own behavior. Put the responsibility where it belongs with, "I'm really sorry I hurt you."

On the other hand, sometimes you just want to reconnect.

To reopen communication with her sister after a falling-out, one woman wrote:

*Dear ———,*

*I know we've said harsh words to each other, but let's call a truce. We haven't spoken in a month and that's long enough.*

*I miss you.*

Too often these days, we haven't the time to reflect, refuel, and find what is deep within us and makes us human. That is what writing does and why it feels so good.

When you put a pen to paper, words spill out. Words from inside that you didn't even know were there. Wonderful words, with meaning.

*More Reasons to Write a Note*

$Sixteen$

$The\ Pleasure\ of\ Stationery$

A friend recently brought me a gift well tuned to my heart—elegant, crisp white correspondence cards engraved at the top with a sunflower. She knew that fine stationery is one of my secret pleasures. I love to touch it. The feel of its weight and texture sends me running for my best pen. "Write someone," it calls out to me.

Why not indulge yourself in the pleasure of stationery that enhances any note you write—and, yes, even inspires you? The guidelines below will help you select the type of stationery that is appropriate for each occasion—and expresses your personality at the same time:

### 1. THINK "ALL-PURPOSE."

The best all-purpose stationery for social notes is correspondence cards for men and foldover notes or correspondence cards for women. These are appropriate for anything from thank-yous to condolence notes. I'm partial to correspondence cards myself. I like the weight of thick stock, and the fact there is limited space in which to write. Writing is less daunting when there is room for only a few lines. If you have more to say, use monarch sheets (which are smaller than letterhead size) or half sheets, which you fold in half.

## 2. PERSONALIZE.

You deserve stationery imprinted with your name or monogram. It makes you feel good. The best-quality paper is 100 percent cotton fiber. It is expensive, but looks wonderful—and it lasts. Decades from now, the recipient of your note can pull it out and remember your thoughtfulness. Similarly, engraving and letterpress are top of the line. If your budget does not permit, however, you can buy good-looking thermographed or printed cards and notepaper at affordable prices from stationery catalogs, online, or in stationery stores. In addition, consider stationery imprinted with a design element, such as a car or a shoe or a flower, rather than your name or monogram. These are available in large card stores and book stores as well as the resources just mentioned. It's fun to have a choice to fit your mood and the situation.

## 3. SELECT COLORS AND STYLES TO EXPRESS YOUR PERSONALITY.

Are you traditional or modern, dignified or adventurous, quiet and shy or a bundle of energy? Are you an aqua paper and magenta ink person? Or do you prefer blue, black, or gray ink, as most men do? What image do you want to project? The answer may vary, depending on whom you're writing to. That's why it's helpful to have more than one stationery choice available.

## 4. CONSIDER THE OCCASION.

Correspondence cards imprinted with your name in red ink—or with a festive design motif—are fine for everything from birthdays to get-well wishes. For condolences, however, stick to stationery with gray, black, or blue ink and/or a design in keeping with the sad occasion.

## 5. REMEMBER THE PEN.

Move beyond ballpoint. The ultimate is a fountain pen to complete the look of your note. If that isn't your style, use a roller ball or a gel pen. They enhance your presentation with a smooth, elegant line. As they glide across the paper, they make writing more enjoyable.

The right tools help you make the right statement about yourself, as well as the recipient. They also multiply the pleasures and satisfaction of writing and sending a message that won't be forgotten.

Keep your stationery handy at home and at work. It's hard enough to write spontaneously without the need to hunt around for something appropriate to write on. Do feel free to get creative in casual situations, too. When a friend of mine moved to another state, she used her new address notification cards as vehicles for personal notes. The card I received included all the vital information, along with these handwritten words scribbled in the margins: "Love the house. The jury is still out on my job. The kids' school is good.

Keeping my fingers crossed. P.S. Are you taking any art courses this year?" Nothing fancy. Just words from a friend that said, "Hello. I'm thinking of you."

Which brings us back to what meaningful notes are all about. They're not about poetry or being profound. They're about being real, reaching out, communicating feelings—and nurturing relationships.